ACTOR'S CHOICE:
Monologues for Women

ACTOR'S CHOICE:

Monologues for Women

Edited by Erin Detrick

Playscripts, Inc.

New York, NY

Actor's Choice: Monologues for Women is published by Playscripts, Inc., 325 West 38th Street, Suite 305, New York, New York, 10018, www.playscripts.com

Cover design by Another Limited Rebellion
Text design and layout by Jason Pizzarello

First Edition: April 2008
10 9 8 7 6 5 4 3 2 1

Editor's Note: In some of the monologues in this book, dialogue or stage directions from the play may have been removed for clarity's sake.

Library of Congress Cataloging-in-Publication Data

Actor's choice : monologues for women / edited by Erin Detrick.
    p. cm.
Summary: "Collection of monologues from the Playscripts, Inc. catalog of plays, representing a variety of American playwrights. The source material for each monologue may be found on the Playscripts website, where nearly the entire text of every play can be read for free. Intended for female actors"--Provided by publisher.
  ISBN-13: 978-0-9709046-4-5 (pbk.)
  1. Monologues. 2. Acting. 3. American drama--20th century. 4. Women--Drama. I. Detrick, Erin, 1981-
  PN2080.A2873 2008
  808.82'45--dc22

                              2007050161

Acknowledgments

First and foremost, this book was made possible by all of the exceptionally talented playwrights who so generously allowed us to include their work. We are deeply appreciative.

Special thanks are due to Jason Pizzarello, Doug Briggs, and Devin McKnight for their monumental contributions to the creation of this book. Thanks also to Noah Scalin, Terry Nemeth, and Arthur Stanley.

Table of Contents

INTRODUCTION

Finding the perfect monologue can be a complicated task. You need a strong, juicy piece of material that will highlight your talents—preferably a piece that hasn't been seen thousands of times already. Furthermore, to fully understand the context of your monologue, you need the play itself at your fingertips to help you prepare. Often that play is impossible to track down. That's where *Actor's Choice* comes in.

We at Playscripts, Inc. have long looked forward to creating a book of monologues drawn from the 1000+ plays we publish. There's a wealth of engaging, dynamic monologues found within those plays—and we're thrilled to make many of them available to you now.

But here's what makes *Actor's Choice* truly unique: For every monologue, you have the option of reading up to 90% of the play it comes from, all from one source, and all for free. Simply visit the Playscripts, Inc. website at *www.playscripts.com*. No longer do you have to waste time searching for a script— the work's already done for you.

On behalf of all the exceptional playwrights represented in this book, we hope that you enjoy these monologues, and that you get the part!

HOW TO USE THIS BOOK

Every monologue in this book is preceded by a brief description that introduces the context. If you'd like to read the play itself, we've made the process simple:

o   Go to the Playscripts, Inc. website: **www.playscripts.com**

o   Run a search for the play title.

o   Click the *Read Sample* link and read away.

o   If you'd like to read the entire play, you may order a book at any time from the Playscripts, Inc. website.

FOREWORD

Confessions of a Broadway Casting Director

I was a year out of college when I went on my first audition in New York City. A friend of mine had left school after getting cast in a national tour, and when one of his fellow actors dropped out, he got me an audition to replace her. I was living in Virginia at the time, so I quickly planned a trip to the big city. I still remember driving over the Verrazano Bridge, nervous with anticipation, and heading to my friend's apartment in Queens. I had picked an outfit, rested my voice, and agonized over which song I should sing. The next day at the audition I walked into the room and sang my song, following all the audition rules I'd learned in college. When I finished I turned expectantly to the casting director. She looked down at my headshot, and then back at me with a slightly confused look and said, "So, who do you—where did…you…come from?" When I explained that my friend was in the tour, it was as if a light went on in her head. She nodded knowingly; my appearance in the casting call suddenly made sense. Even with my lack of big city audition experience, I knew this was not a good sign. I had clearly made some rookie mistakes, I didn't get the part, and I left New York feeling I had blown my big chance.

I moved to New York City shortly thereafter and only lasted a year before I gave up acting. Fortunately, I found another great vocation—on the other side of the table as a casting director. If I knew then what I know now, that first audition would have gone a lot differently.

I truly believe that actors have one of the hardest jobs around. Just look at the audition situation alone—actors have to be charming but not arrogant, vulnerable but not needy, friendly but not so friendly that the people on the other side of the table start to get scared. They have to be interesting, brilliant, moving, memorable, and right for the part. Often all in three minutes or less.

Some audition tips are obvious. Then again, I've still seen each of the following scenarios on several occasions, so perhaps these tips bear repeating...

o Don't stand too close to the person behind the table. Firstly because it's an invasion of personal space, and secondly because a little distance helps us with perspective.

o If there is a reader present for your audition, please don't excessively touch or molest them. Unfortunately, I've seen it happen often and it's uncomfortable for everyone.

o If your audition involves reading a scene, don't worry about memorizing lines unless you've been asked to. I'd much rather watch an actor refer to pages and be in the moment, than watch them mentally panic over what the next line is.

o Always second-guess the use of props, and the amount of the audition you spend lying on, crawling across, rolling around on, or throwing yourself to the floor. You don't have to tell me which special skills on your resume make you really right for this and how much you want this part. I know you want this part, as I assume you wouldn't be here if you didn't.

o And finally, unless we know each other, it's probably best to leave your personal life out of the audition room. I've had people tell me about everything from brain tumors to painful divorces. And while I'd happily hear about your life over a cup of coffee, the audition room is not the right forum for it.

What many actors don't know is that the people on the other side of the table are actually on your side. We desperately want you to be our answer. We want you to be brilliant just as badly as you want to be brilliant. The best auditions I've seen have been when actors come in the room simply as themselves. Don't waste your energy trying to figure out who or what you think we want you to be. Be who you are. It's always more interesting. Because as much as this is going to sound like your mother talking, there is no one out there like you. No one brings exactly the same things to a scene or monologue that you do. So find out what it is that you are able to relate to in a character and explore it. And when you do, figure out where the vulnerability is. In every audition, you've got to create a compelling character. Finding the vulnerability means that I get to see exactly what that character is really feeling, even if it's ugly or embarrassing. And that is always fascinating to watch.

The monologues in this book do half of the work for you. They are fresh, truthful, and interesting, not to mention brand-new material (which means I won't be comparing you to the girl/guy who used your same monologue five people ago). If you can deliver a monologue that is genuine, natural, and has vulnerability to it, even if you're not right for whatever I might be casting that day, I will put you in my "Remember Them" file and keep you in mind for other opportunities down the road. In the long run, so much of casting has to do with tiny details that are beyond your control. So do yourself a favor. Show up, give a truthful performance, and let the rest go. You are enough.

Again, if only I had known that, who knows how my first audition in New York would have turned out...!

Kate Schwabe
Associate Casting Director, Jim Carnahan Casting
Roundabout Theatre Company, New York City

16 SPELLS TO CHARM THE BEAST

Lisa D'Amour

Lillian, a mature housewife in crisis over the recent writing of her will, is being stalked by an ugly Beast who lives across town in a crappy apartment. The Beast stands behind her, holding a paper snowflake dress he has made especially for her. Lillian fears the Beast, and tries to insult him and make him leave.

LILLIAN. Millicent? Millicent dear is that you? My dear I am so glad you are here you are the one who enters without knocking you are the one who I let in to all my fragile little dioramas. I am glad you are here Millicent for I have a suspicion I must tell you about a suspicion I fear no one else will give any credence to and here is that suspicion: There is a Beast who watches me. This beast, a bona fide beast, lives in an apartment several miles South of here. It is a crappy apartment with inadequate light, nothing like this apartment. He first started ogling me through a small window with a very expensive telescope that is the only thing of value that he owns. Everything else he owns is either crappy or not really his. From the very first time he started ogling me I could feel the lens of his telescope squeaking across my body like a greasy fingernail. He clings to that telescope even though the building next door makes it entirely impossible for him to locate me in the scope. Now that ogling from afar is not an option, I fear he is planning a visit. I fear that he is operating under the false assumption that he has figured out certain things that I want that *I myself* am not aware that I want. Ha! Ha! As though he has some divine right to assume such things! As though as a result of this knowledge he might bestow upon me the perfect gift, a delicate, intricate, handmade gift, a gift that will compel me to saw through my own sternum, extract my own cold, cruel heart and devour it whole. As if, after this grotesque act of auto-cannibalism the two of us will gaze into my sawed open ribcage and watch a new heart grow, a heart as tiny and fragrant as a primrose

1

and as dear as an infant's palm, as though the two of us might then rejoice at my generating this sweet, beneficent new heart and stroll together, together down the primrose path through the new fallen snow, la la la pocket full of posies la la, as though by new heart might cajole me to look his into his wet, beastly eyes and call him "Jonathan" or even "Jonathan Keene." But you Millicent, you know that some hearts are genetically cold and cruel and unchangeable, and that I would never, ever, even in a thousand million eons accept any gift from a steaming, stinking, rotting *Beast*.

16 Spells to Charm the Beast

Lisa D'Amour

Lillian, a mature housewife in crisis over the recent writing of her will, is being stalked by an ugly Beast who lives across town in a crappy apartment. Towards the end of the play, she has an epiphany about the nature of her existence. She speaks to her husband Ned, her neighbor Millicent Hiccup and to herself.

LILLIAN. Before your eyes, in This Realm, I am a housewife. But there is another Realm, a Realm at first imagined but eventually Real, called Realm of Clear Seeing. When Viewed from the Other Realm, I am not simply a bored and sophisticated metropolitan housewife, staring out of a window, contemplating a view, but something more like a Revered Eyeball, an Eyeball charged with observing the Way Things Really Are. And believe me I have observed. I have spent hours gazing out this window, entire days focusing on a single object, trying to look deep into its being, past the illusion of static, physical form, hoping that I might observe something that filters through me to the other realm, where the substantial things shimmer with a clarity that we will never know. Now in the midst of all this observing, my life has taken shape around me. I married you, Ned—

We moved into this spacious, rent controlled apartment, we conceived, together, a daughter which we named Norma, which daughter I tried to love, and indeed did love, but somehow, perhaps because of my role as Observer, I failed to establish any sort of bond with her, and her life has gone on. And you Ned, present charade accepted, have tried in your honest yet flawed manner to love and honor me and make a life with me, you have sweet-talked me into pursuing activities that might cheer me up, such as sculpting the clay obelisks that remain, still in the closet. And I do appreciate your efforts, Ned, I do, but the problem remains that I have played the role of Eyeball for so many years now, that I can no longer distinguish the essential objects from the non-essential ones—a husband and ball of twine will often exist in the same category for me, for example—and since I can no longer qualify any of the objects, animal or mineral, which surround me, I can only conclude that I DO NOT EXIST, and therefore find it impossible, or at the very least absurd, to engage in interpersonal relationships, or to consider the issue of my "tangible personal property" much less the distribution thereof.

ACT A LADY

Jordan Harrison

Lorna grew up in a Prohibition-era Midwestern town and left for Hollywood to be a make-up specialist. She has been hired by her old local theatre to do the make-up for their play. In the play, all of the characters, including the females, will be played by men.

LORNA. The first start to being pretty is powder for that nice even tone. Don't know nobody who gotta nice even tone without the helpa powder 'cept maybe the Chinawoman who works down in the laundry. Asked her once how she gets such fine even tone and she touched my cheek—her hand just shot out from behind the counter and stretched my cheek-skin between her thumb and pointerfinger like that, and she said: "Peaches and cream." Peaches and cream is all she said but I knew somehow that meant "You're all right, Lorna—you be happy with what you got." That was nice. But that's a whole other story.

First start to being pretty is powder and you use the powder puff here, puff puff puff anywhere and everywhere but 'specially wher'ever it's—darn it, darn it. Darn it I shoulda started you all off with *shaving.* Shaving for the boys, gotta shave real close first or else you'll end up looking like you're some kinda sideshow act let out on the loose—which is okay if that's what you want but that's not what we want. Illusion we want. Elegant we want. *Ladies* we want.

I know, I'm a dreamer, I know, that's what they call me. But I think when we get all your wives and sisters and momfolk lined up opening night they're gonna see I've been dreaming real. Now, third step after shave 'n powder is gonna be your eyes. Big big eyes to put Pickford to shame. You do wanna look pretty, right fellas?

ALL THOSE VIOLENT SWEATERS

Ruth Margraff

Edith talks on the phone next to a small table with a centerpiece. She has an extremely long braid that wraps around her as if she were planted there in an extremely sedentary "still life."

EDITH. *(On the phone.)* Hello is this Victoria Secret? Hello is this London? It's Ohio? well, you sound sort've British, no, oh no, I think your bras are terrible, your clothes are terrible and everybody in there is a bag of bones. Nobody's going to look like that if they buy that underwear from you, I don't mean extra large, who knows the way you size those skimpy little, shoestring…on page 6. Okay my question is. I could BE a customer you don't—you don't know that—this is what I WILL buy, listen to me—sell me what you CAN sell is the house on page six, I'd like that house, I'd like it with the lamp, the airbrushed ocean, plastic surgery, who knows, we all look pretty when we're lacy. Give me the house, I'm telling you it's real estate and lingerie and you're in business. I'll buy the wonder bra, the miracle—the white zinfandel and the. Sell the whole entire, the deluxe, is what I'm saying. I won't even charge you for the secret. You don't know what I can-NOT afford and that's the phoniest fakest—no you HAVE to talk to me, I might BECOME a customer, I might BECOME unsatisfied with your performance, okay then I will buy the bra. Page six. Okay…okay…okay…never mind.

*(*EDITH *hangs up phone. Beat. Dials, picks it up again.)*

Hello is this Tweeds? Hello. I just have one quick question and it's silly but page 29 okay the girl is wearing heather grey for one thing, but the house that's off like in the distance and there's puddles all around her? Well I think I've been there, right there where she's standing, by that house, the upstairs window, I can't tell because

Actor's Choice: Monologues for Women

she's inside, you might have faked something, you can fake things like that I suppose but those are really puddles on page 29. You've got the puddles and the heather grey and then the house, it's good. It's worth it, going through a lot of bullshit in my mail to get to this picture. It is really getting to me right now. *(Sucks her breath in.)* I feel like I've been there and she's selling something to me, it's right here, I have this house, see I don't know where it came from but it comes into my head and sits there and I can't remember it or anything, I don't know where it is. I make my sweaters, I make all of them myself, I mean I knit them. *(Crying.)* But I like to see what you do and I like this one, it's nice. I like the little boxes right beside the sweaters where you show the texture of it up close, and your stitches are, your stitches… *(Sobbing almost.)* I just really like those little boxes. That's what you should really sell I think.

(EDITH *hangs up phone.)*

ALOHA, SAY THE PRETTY GIRLS

Naomi Iizuka

Wendy has started dating girls. She wonders why people scramble for simple companionship rather then waiting for happiness.

WENDY. why? i mean, why is it that all of a sudden everybody you know starts wanting to get married and have babies, and everything that comes along with getting married and having babies? is it just some kinda instinct, some kinda lizard brain instinct, like turtles or lemmings or moose in spring, or is it maybe this sudden awareness that kicks in that you're not getting any younger, and someday you're maybe gonna get sick and old and then maybe you're gonna die—well not maybe—you are, i mean you are gonna die, we're all gonna die, that's the deal—but whatever, maybe you're having trouble with that concept, or maybe you just don't want to be doing all of that stuff alone, and i think you can think of this in terms of musical chairs, i think it's actually a lot like musical chairs, and so there you are, having spent most of your twenties playing this game of musical chairs, and suddenly it's like you turn twenty-eight, twenty-nine, and somebody turns the music off, and it gets really quiet in the room, and you look around, and the thing is, right, there's not enough chairs to go around, somebody's gonna be left chairless, somebody's gonna get screwed, and before you know it, everybody's scrambling around, looking for a place to park their ass, and people are getting knocked to the ground, and there's shoving happening, and elbows in the eyes, and it's ugly, ok, it's really ugly, but you're right in there, you're in the fray, and so finally you get yourself a chair, and you're happy because you're like seated, but then before too long, you know, you turn to look at the people sitting next to you, and it's like, who are you again? and what am i doing sitting next to you? do i really want to be sitting next to you? and also, this chair, i'm not so sure about this chair, i mean maybe i don't even want to be seated, maybe i want to stand. so now, ok, this is the thing: i used to fuck guys, and now i fuck girls, and i'm personally very happy about that little change of scenery, but you'd think, you know, that it's a different thing, that this whole musical chair thing, it's a guy/girl thing, and now that i'm doing this girl/girl thing, the whole musical chair thing, it's not going to be the same thing, but it is, it's like the exact same thing, it's like musical chairs only with different chairs.

AMERICAN KLEPTO

Allison Moore

A woman in her early 20s stands outside her boyfriend's car on a road in Arizona. He caught her with a piece of petrified wood that she stole from the national park they just visited. She attempts to explain.

WOMAN. I don't know how it got here. It's just a piece of wood. Okay, petrified wood. Don't do that. This entire trip you've been judging me, 700 miles and now you judge my moisturizer, my hiking boots, my cell phone—which, I might add, you were very happy to use yesterday when the tire blew and you remembered you never replaced the freakin spare. Who I am is suddenly wrong out here. I mean, why does it matter if I want to buy some moccasins or a leather hairclip? Why does it matter if the stitching isn't authentic to the tribes of the area? Why does it matter if I'll never wear them when we get home? Did it ever occur to you that I am trying to connect? That this might be a profound expression of engagement? But everything I touch, you say Don't touch that! Don't buy that! If you buy that hairclip, you're supporting the rape of a culture all so that white middle class tourists can go home with a souvenir—and yes I know "white" is a construct!

I am a good person. I am not an exploiter, or a thief, or. I mean, where did you get that pen? Do you know? When was the last time you actually went out and bought a shitty disposable pen? But here it is, on your dashboard. How did it get there? I'll tell you: *You took it.* Junk drawers across the country are filled with pens like this because we take them. That's what Americans do, we take pens, from everywhere. From grocery stores, from gas stations, from work. If you took a computer that would be theft, but no one cares if you take a pen, or some paperclips, they order in bulk. But technically, you're stealing. You are a thief. You have stolen pens. That's what we're talking about here.

I know there was a sign, I know it's Federally protected land, but. When I was a kid I found a ton of fossils at Canyon Lake—I'm talking close to a hundred of them, little snails and water plants. No one ever said You're decontextualizing our geological history. They said Wow! These are heavy! And let me tell you something, if I hadn't found them, someone else would have. They'd probably be selling them right now in a gift shop somewhere.

I know! We should put signs everywhere, not just in National Parks. "Take only pictures, leave only foot prints" on banners like corporate mission statements in office buildings everywhere. Prosecute little girls picking flowers, jail time for arrogant asshole eco-motherfuckers with stolen pens!

(Beat.)

I swear to God I didn't mean to take it, I don't remember taking it. I remember standing in the middle of the desert thinking how it reminded me of Gettysburg in winter, how the petrified wood looked like corpses lying in the sand. And you said It really does look painted, like you're walking around inside one of those paintings we saw in Taos. And we couldn't stop touching that trunk because it looked like it was decaying, it had been decaying, but it had stopped, frozen by the sun and time. And I picked up a little piece and poured water on it to bring out the colors, and. I don't want to rape anyone, I just wanted the goddamn hairclip.

(She examines the piece of petrified wood.)

It's not even a very pretty one.

ANNA BELLA EEMA

Lisa D'Amour

Irene, a hermetic single mother, is about to be evicted from her trailer home. Her precocious ten year old daughter, Anna Bella, recently created a new girl out of mud: Anna Bella Eema. This is Anna Bella Eema's first night in the house. One speaks as Irene.

ONE. Now it is the three of us on the pull out couch. Anna Bella lies on my right side and Anna Bella Eema on my left. It's the only way we can all sleep. Anna Bella curls up beneath one of my arms and Anna Bella Eema beneath the other. They make sweet eyes at each other for awhile, but eventually, they are quiet.

Their breathing makes me think about the ocean. I went to the ocean once when I was a little girl. It was a dark night. I flew there on the back of a swan. The moon was out. The ocean was dark with white waves surfacing like the baby teeth of little girls. The swan says "This is the ocean. You are on the bottom." I laugh and bury my face in his feathers. "That is not me," I say. "Those are other little girls." The moon speaks "You are on the bottom. And the water is so heavy you cannot move." I wave my arms: "Look at me! I am moving!" And the swan says: "Are you really moving?" And the moon says: "Are you really moving?" And I realize that I am not. Really moving. I can feel the water pressing down. Immobilizing me. I am at the bottom of the ocean. It is dark and quiet and the swan is drowned beside me. The water presses down and I feel a tentacle slide around my ankle. I am on the bottom of the ocean.

I am on the pull-out couch. Anna Bella and Anna Bella Eema have wrapped themselves around me in their sleep. They cling to me and breathe.

I have never been to the ocean.

Anna Bella Eema

Lisa D'Amour

Anna Bella's mother recently died very young after the two of them were evicted from their trailer home because of highway construction. Her mother had an acute sense of the supernatural, and perhaps the soul of a wolf. Anna Bella has been placed in a foster home. In this scene, Anna Bella Eema, a girl Anna Bella made out of mud, comes to say goodbye. Two speaks as Anna Bella.

TWO. I do well in school, to everyone's surprise. They imagine I will be unruly. What they forget is that the wild creature's first and most important means of self-defense is its ability to adapt.

I miss my mother. She is extraordinarily gone. Only her books remain. I read them all, twice, and then I bring them to the library and donate them to their collection. My new mother does not think this is wise. She says I should keep reminders. But I want to limit my possessions. I plan to travel some day.

Many, many, many weeks after I moved into my new home and started school, I was visited by Anna Bella Eema, the little girl I made that day out of plain earth behind the trailer home. I was lying in my bed, just starting to fall asleep, when I heard a rapping on my window pane. I had an instinctual knowledge of who it was. I opened the window and she crawled in bed with me. It felt good, even though she was, of course, very very muddy. I held her close to my chest. She nestled her muddy nose into my now-plump breasts. She made me laugh out loud.

(She laughs out loud.)

Then she looked deep into my eyes, touched her nose to my nose and said:

One. Two. Three.

And then she laughed out loud. And I took my right hand and touched my fingers to her lips and reached up and closed both of her eyelids and she was gone.

(TWO takes a moment to consider the audience.)

Here we are.

Some days I feel I am completely new. I have killed many things and seen many new places. And other days, quiet days, I become very aware of my little bird soul, still fluttering around in the cage of my ribs. The same little bird that the fox saw so clearly, the same little bird my mother felt fluttering in her womb. The same little bird that sprouted these fine white teeth.

(She bares her teeth.)

Highway 20 now cuts right through the heart of town. The speed limit is 60 miles per hour. It takes approximately 3 seconds to drive over the square of land that once was our trailer park. It's like it was never even there.

APHRA DOES ANTWERP

Liz Duffy Adams

Antwerp, 1666. The witty and adventurous Aphra Behn—poet, Royalist spy, and soon to become the first professional female playwright—is on a mission and in desperate straits.

APHRA.
Money! Guilders, sterling, shillings, dough!
Say what you will, God knows I need it so.
The higher things in life I might prefer
To muse upon, profoundly to refer.
I might delight to think upon the joys
Of love, or poetry, the pretty toys
That noble minds do use to pass the time
To season troubled reason with sweet rhyme.
But damn! (to vent vexation with a curse)
For me the base woes of the empty purse.
To costly Antwerp did I wend my way
To serve my King and country as a spy.
And now that I'm ensconced here in this inn
Racking up a bill that spells ruin
The men I trust to keep me here afloat
Have vouchsafed me not yet a single note!
The landlord just this morning dropped a hint;
I think the words he used were "lying bint."
If something can't be done to keep him sweet
I may yet find myself out on the street.
And worst of all, the man I'm here to see
Is so far none so eager to see me.
No one is more suspicious or more shy
Than double agents meeting on the sly.
But if the rogue won't come across and soon

With info worth at least a copper spoon
My spy masters will never yet agree
To pay my bills and passage 'cross the sea
Back to London, my beloved home
Whence, if I'm again, I'll never roam.
Oh, Aphra, use your wits, for what they're worth;
Money's sure as good a spur as mirth.

A Trois

Barry Hall

B, her persona shifting to that of a prostitute, describes the advantages of her occupation over other jobs. She discusses the interesting "clients" she meets and the benefits of possessing acting experience all while seducing the person she's talking to.

B. What can I say? What do you want me to say? It beats working? The money's good? Yeah, sometimes. Better than nine to five. And the *people* you meet! I'm not saying you'll meet the President of the United States—though I wouldn't rule it out—but—well, just the other night, do you know who I met at this very bar? I met a client—"client"—from Bismarck who was the *biggest* seller of industrial drill bits in the *whole* of Southwestern North Dakota.

Beats working.

Oh, and this guy—this client—(that's another thing—the *stories* you hear)—told me all about his experience in the war (the Gulf War, remember that one?)—"just like playing a video game"—and how he came back and married his childhood sweetheart and fought to survive in the untamed Southwestern North Dakota industrial drill bit jungle, which eventually brought him…to me. Business. Travel. They get lonely.

I have a master's in philosophy. Well, I'm really just a semester short. But I usually leave that part out. Makes for a better story.

I did some acting in college. Ms. Kinghorn, my—business manager, says "the theater is the best school for" our—profession. I had the lead in one show—*Our Town*. Well, not *Our Town*, actually, but—makes for a better story.

Acting. That's it, basically. That's all there is to it. You play the role. Whatever that may be. Whatever may be—*required*. Shy. Delicate.

Brazen. Dominant. Vulnerable. Aggressive. Demure. Mysterious. Honest.

I *have* been honest with you, haven't I? Isn't that what you wanted?

You know, I have a bottle of wine in my room. We could speak so much more—*freely* there.

Oh, of course. Of *course*. Just leave everything up to me. Don't worry about a thing. Room 326. I'll leave the door unlocked.

A Backward Glance

Julie McKee

A heavy-drinking divorcee, Evelyn, complains about her son to a neighbor's young daughter, who is secretly in love with him.

EVELYN. I mean she's a nice girl. Her mother says that she's never been any trouble at all. A fine girl. And I'm sure she's right. But! But! It can't keep a clean kitchen, let alone a clean house. Terrible. The training that girl must have had... Now I know your mother's as neat as a pin, and she never trained you to be a slut.

Second of all she doesn't even bother to iron her pillowcases and doesn't even bother to hide the fact. No. Says she's got better things to do.

Thirdly, she's the type of person, who after using public transport, will come right into your home and sit on your bed. I just can't stand those sort of people.

But you haven't heard the worst! The worst thing of all was...cause I had to stay the night at her house, under protest of course because she thought I was too drunk to drive. Ha!

I mean they're living together she and he, don't ask me, just don't ask, but that's the way everyone does it nowadays. I don't say anything, I keep my mouth shut. No-one wants my opinion anyway.

So I go for dinner, you know, cooks really well, nice manners, and all that, which of course are extremely important, especially in this day and age... Where was I? Oh. But!, I had to ask for two towels. Now I ask you. How did she think I was going to manage with only one towel?

Yes. I mean to say. You've got to have one towel for the upper part of your body and one for the lower part don't you? Dirty. She's dirty. I hate to say it, but it's true. Shame really 'cos I like her. Very bright. Comes from a lovely family. Plenty of money as I said, but of course that's not everything as you well know.

Oh! and you must know them, they're Jews too! I mean we hardly got through discussing how many of you there are. Father's in sacks or burlap or something or other. Fisher's the name. Marilyn Fisher.

BEE-LUTHER-HATCHEE

Thomas Gibbons

Libby Price, an elderly African-American woman, has spent her life wandering through the South. She describes an encounter on a train.

LIBBY. ...I heard the door of the car open and the conductor come in to collect the tickets.

I sat real still and tried to be invisible. Usually that ain't too hard with white folks. Except when it comes to money—then you shine like the sun.

He stopped next to me and said, Can I see your ticket? I don't have one, I said. Not lookin' at him. You can buy one from me, he said. He had a nice voice. I said, I don't have the money.

Come with me, he said. Come on. His voice still sounded nice, but there was somethin' different in it.

All the people in the car were starin' at me, I could tell. No one was talkin'. I stood up and followed him all the way up the aisle into the next car...the kind that had private compartments.

Please, mister, I said. I know I done wrong. Just let me get off at the next stop.

He grabbed my wrist and started lookin' through the windows of the compartments. You're hurtin' me, I told him. He opened a door and pushed me into an empty compartment. He pulled the shade down on the window. Then he turned around and hit me. Not real hard...just enough to *let me know.*

And he said, Since you can't buy a ticket, you'll have to earn your ride.

BLOODY THANKSGIVING

Brooke Berman

It's Thanksgiving, Nina has just started her period and her grandmother refuses to take her to the store for tampons. While walking to the store, Nina considers her upbringing.

NINA. These are tampons. You stick them up inside yourself and they stop up the flow of blood. It's kind of an interesting metaphor, only I'm not sure what for. I was not able to even use these until I was 22 years old. Nobody in my family told me about them, so I assumed they were meant for someone else and I just used those pads, the ones that stick inside your underwear. This is probably grossing you out a little. I don't know. I don't have a very clear monitor in terms of what is polite conversation and what isn't. My fondest memories of my mother involve her naked in the kitchen stuffing a turkey. So let's just say I don't have good social grace boundaries. I had bad parenting— Isn't that just a great excuse for everything?

I don't usually go home for the holidays. Certainly not since my mother died. But this year something felt like it might be different. I felt a sense of…possibility. Like anything was possible and like maybe it could be different with us.

Fuck that shit.

BUT WHO'S COUNTING

Larry Loebell

A stylish, successful architect with a prodigious sex life brings home a geeky guy to be her 2000th partner on the eve of the new millennium.

WOMAN. Time wise, it is like 9:35 on the last day of 1999. Let's say this black box is the living room of my apartment. I have very cool furniture, befitting an award-winning mid-career architect, which is what I am. I've got a niche—law firm design, so I mostly do interior space in large buildings. My living room reflects my taste: Roche-Bobois chairs, this magnificent antique lacquered table I picked up on my last trip to Japan, hand printed Italian drapes, a huge Sara Steele watercolor of an endangered orchid over the sofa, Noguchi lanterns, and Dale Chihuly blown glass nesting bowls as accents. We're in that luxury condo development they built on pier 41 over the Delaware. And I've got the best unit. Through that window I have an unobstructed view of Camden Aquarium, all lit up tonight in blues—meaning clear skies tomorrow. And back there in my bedroom, a man I picked up less than a half an hour ago at a New Year's Eve party at Egypt on Delaware Avenue is waiting for me. But really, I'm not in a rush.

In a few minutes, when we're finished talking, you're gonna leave and I'm going to go through that door and into my bedroom to give that man the fuck of his life. He's getting a little nervous right now wondering where I am, because I've been gone a while. He watched me get into this outfit and now he's wondering if he's made a mistake coming home with me. He's thinking, she looked pretty normal in the bar. She didn't seem crazy. I want to give him some time to get used to the idea that something special is going to happen to him—to both of us—tonight.

I spotted him right away at Egypt. The party was revving up. The DJs were cranking out a nice mix of techno, trance, jungle, ambient, with an occasional oldie thrown in to slow things down. I'd been dancing with a succession of guys when this one caught my eye. He was standing alone and watching the dancers, and I saw him just sort of shrinking. There are certain people who should never go to parties alone. You gotta have the energy to keep yourself in the flow. This guy, I watched him retreat to a table near the wall. He looked all right, a web rat in Dockers and plaid, kinda cute in an "I-know-all-the-hidden-apps-on-the-Palm-Pilot" sort of way. So I watched him. I tried to figure out why he'd come. This clearly wasn't a bar guy. I decided he'd been dumped recently, and that this was his first time out in a while, like he'd just decided there was no way he was going to spend New Year's Eve alone. Particularly this New Year's. But he also wasn't going to spend it with any of his old friends because they'd just remind him of Ellen or Mindy or whoever she was, so he picked this place out of the phone book or he maybe heard about it from some other geek at the pharmaceutical company where he hand-holds the Luddites at the I.T. help desk, or he noticed an ad in the City Paper while was flipping toward the personals—White Professional Female, huge mammaries, desires recently dumped geeky guy for sex; willing to let you act out your retribution fantasies against your ex on me—hope really does spring eternal, you know, and so he drove in from Tredyffrin or wherever. In situations where you have to make judgments about people quickly, you often have to do it without the benefit of back story. I'm pretty good at making them up. You'd be amazed how often I get it right.

Anyway, he struck me as one of those guys who never really feels confident, which I actually like because men who swagger in my experience often turn out to be creeps, so I came on to him. Very sweetly. I wasn't wearing this. He bought me a drink. We talked. We danced a couple of times. He wasn't a very good dancer, surprise surprise, but he was earnest. And his body was okay. Better than I expected. I suggested maybe we go someplace quieter for a private celebration. He thought I meant a quieter bar.

Now, I guess you should know that the reason I know he's waiting patiently in there is because he's tied to the bed. Well, chained, actually. I'm partial to sixteen gauge double weld, with figure 8 links, because they're smooth and relatively light. Also, sixteen fits through the rings on both of the cuff sets I own. And it doesn't look like something out of a Roger Corman babes-in-prison-with-chainsaws flick. It's light duty, like for chaining newspaper boxes to street signs so they won't get stolen. But it does the trick.

I got introduced to bondage a few years back by a guy I let tie me up one night. He was a guy who used to work in my firm, another architect. His niche was parking structures. I knew this guy had a kink because he liked to talk about it over lunch. I wasn't sure he was telling the truth. I thought he was trying to look hip to the gay guys, so I decided to call his bluff. Turns out he's a pretty good top. He's one of those guys who likes to narrate, so he got a kick out of training me, who likes to listen. Not that you'd know that from how many words I'm letting you get in edgewise, but take my word. I was happy to be the bottom—at least once.

This guy, this Tom with the okay body and the pen protector personality and the surprisingly big dick who is in my bedroom—Rothman is it? I need to ask him again—this Harry is my 2000th fuck. My millennium orgasm.

CLEVELAND

Mac Wellman

A mother tells her daughter the story of her father's death for the first time.

MOTHER. Well. All right. We were in New York for the party congress. We had just met the Mayor of Cleveland. Of course he wasn't a Trotskyist. He was far too fashionable for that. A fine, big man he was, with a fine, big, round head. He said to your father: "Fine work. That report on solid waste." Then he introduced himself to me. It was an awkward moment because, of course, your father had no idea what the mayor was talking about. It seems he was at the wrong hotel. "We're Trotskyists." We said. "My apologies." He said. "May I buy you a drink?" And he did. One of those elegant little sidewalk cafés. Lovely.

(A sad moment.)

We were sitting on the sidewalk. Or, rather, at a table on the sidewalk. And your father leaned over to make a point and spilled his espresso. As he moved forward with the saucer in his other hand the heel snapped off his shoe and well he slid back into the chair. Of course the coffee got over everyone. And the chair leg broke and, it was quite remarkable, he did a nice, little, wholly unintentional back-flip into the street. I shall never forget the sight of his shoes, the soles of them, as they lifted high into the air. He was trying to save the cup, poor dear. But it shattered in the street, and then the first car ran over it. And the saucer which had been undamaged miraculously up to that point. He was a quite fastidious man. The second car ran over your father. Quite a large car. A limo, I think. "My word." Said the mayor. What a strange thing to say. Of course he was dead. Your father, I mean. That's about it. More coffee.

CRUMBLE
(LAY ME DOWN, JUSTIN TIMBERLAKE)

Sheila Callaghan

Barbara awkwardly attempts to comfort her estranged niece, Janice, through girl-talk a year after the death of Janice's father.

BARBARA. Janice honey… Mommy says your hair is wire and your breath is napalm. Mommy says you asked for seven really strange gifts this year. Your poor Mommy is so worried. You know how she gets. You don't want to give Mommy a lobotomy, do you? Are you thinking of Christmas last year? You can talk about it. Hm?

Oh, I think I know… I was eleven once too… I had a Secret Crush. Mickey Forinelli. Never told a soul, not even my best friend. I watched him eat lunch every day. That boy could eat… do you watch boys eat.

(JANICE *says nothing.*)

It's all right, it's perfectly healthy. Boys. Feelings about boys? Watching the poster of the boy on your wall come alive at night? He floats over to you like a question mark, lays his boy hands on all your new parts…

You don't have to answer, your face says it all. Well, now we're talking, this is Girl Talk. Good good. Feels good to talk. Clears the noggin like a blast of freon. Ahhh.

(*Silence. And more silence.* BARBARA *is at an utter loss.*)

How about it, buddy? Is there a boy out there in Boyland gotcha down? Tell me tell me tell me…

DEBT

Seth Kramer

Molly, a mistress who dominates men, confesses her love for the one man who she can't resist.

MOLLY. I don't pretend to know everything about men. Not all of them. Just a few. A certain kind of man. I know him after five minutes in a room together. That restless thing. That wandering eye. I know him, right there, as soon as he looks at me. A little work, a little interest, a little contact and I know exactly what comes next.

(Beat.)

It's power knowing you can take someone away from whatever life they're living. Knowing even more that they want that. Want you to take them.

(Pause.)

When she's right there. When she's in the same room. Sometimes it's worth doing just for the look on her face. Five minutes for me and three hours for them. Fighting about it later. It's power.

(Pause.)

I can find that type every time I walk out the door but you… I've never found anyone who can make me feel like you do. You're like a drug for me. A feeling that…I can't even describe it…when I'm fucking them, when I feel them under my body… I think of you. You're the voice I hear when they say my name.

(Pause.)

Today, when I walked in and saw you standing in the living room, I almost—almost…

(Beat.)

I thought I was dreaming—that you couldn't be real. My legs actually shook. So many times—for months after you left—I'd come home hoping to find some trace of you—a sign you'd come back—your coat hanging in the closet, your keys on the table. Anything. I waited and waited hoping, worrying, doubting myself…

(Beat.)

And now here you are.

(Beat.)

I'm glad you came back, baby. It's been so long. I started to think… Think I'd lost you… That you'd found someone else. I couldn't deal with that.

(Beat.)

You should stay here tonight. It's just been so long… The way you know me. My body. We can take a shower together. Whatever you want. Alright?

(Pause.)

I'll help you get the money. Everything will be fine now. Now that you're back.

(Pause.)

I know I can help you.

Dirty Little Secrets

Jeffrey M. Jones

Lisa(Marie) gives an interview, in which she reminisces about her world-famous father, who performed in Las Vegas and was found dead in the the bathroom of his Memphis home. Unlike most monologues, this is (a) delivered presentationally, as to a reporter or television camera, and (b) composed of intimate, autobiographic material which the speaker has carefully shaped in advance, and performs with the aim of appearing spontaneous. It is all true, but it is also completely synthetic; the public manufacture of personal history.

LISA. Sometimes, I close my eyes

And I can see my Daddy standing there, with that big old grin…

Forever young and strong…

Cause even though my Daddy may be gone,

I just thank God he could leave me with such beautiful memories.

I mean, it was a miracle, the life I had…

Cause my mom—she was in stuff—but we had an ordinary life-style,

And then once a year, I'd get whisked off on this magic carpet ride—I mean, it was—it was a fairy tale—to the point where sometimes I didn't know if I was dreaming.

Like one time my Daddy just called up in the middle of school—hadda go to the Principal's office, it was totally embarrassing—there's Daddy on the phone, going, "Lisa, honey," you know, the way he did, "Lisa, honey, you ever seen snow?" (like, Dad—this is Southern California, Dad…) He's going, "You just stay right there, I'm coming get you."

So then we just jet off to Aspen, I'm riding on snowmobiles, making these snowmen and so forth, you know—so, that was *snow*...

And like whenever I'd go up Vegas, My god—I mean one time he had like six slot machines in the suite—or like another time it was cute little puppies, little Saint Bernard's—or like you'd open a drawer, it'd be full of jewels—you'd open the closet, it'd be full of furs—you never knew what to expect...

Or like, when we'd go back to Memphis—I remember like one time they had this amusement park back there called Liberty Land—and it was a pretty big deal—so Daddy decided we'd all take it over for the day, just me and him and the entourage—I mean, and I was in heaven, I got to ride on the carousel whenever I wanted to, go on the roller-coaster, play all the games—and the guys in the entourage—you know, Red and the other guys—they were all riding around the bumper cars, and they let Daddy smash into them, cause they all knew how much he loved smashing into stuff.

So then of course I wanted to start smashin' into stuff, so the next time I come back to Memphis, Daddy let me drive around in the golf-cart, and I just went crazy, I was running into walls, and driving over flowerbeds and so forth—I just set everybody to scampering...

And I had this totally cool bed my Daddy had bought me, we called it the hamburger bed, cause it was round, and it had this fuzzy brown bedspread—I don't know, so I guess it was a fuzzy hamburger—but I sure loved that bed, I really, I did...

And then one night, I woke up, you know, in the middle of the night,

And there was all this commotion going on...

People was sayin' he was dead, and I shouldn't go into the bathroom, cause that's where he was, and—Ginger I mean, she was crying, everybody was crying and...

You know, that afternoon, Mom showed right up and took me back home and...

That was it, that was the end of it.

Never even saw my bed again, you know?....

And that was, I was nine, I was nine years old.

DIRTY LITTLE SECRETS

Jeffrey M. Jones

Debbie recounts the events surrounding her marriage to Michael, an international celebrity with a peculiar interest in little boys. She considers herself one of his biggest fans, and has agreed to carry his child. The monologue is derived from articles in the tabloid press, and can be imagined as an extended, one-sided phone conversation with a distant friend.

DEBBIE. Why did I even believe him?

I said, "You're in Australia, Mike!"

He said, "Yeah, but I wanna get married, Debbie—right now, Debbie—hurry!"

So I got on the next plane out, and I flew like eighteen hours straight, and I mean, they're not even supposed to let you on the plane after the seventh month…

And then I get to the hotel, you know, I'm like totally wiped out, I mean, and *nobody's* been there to meet me at the airport, I had to take a taxi…

And then they say "Oh, you're in separate bedrooms, because Michael's little friend is staying with him."

And I'm like, "Michael, why are you doing this to me? Why are you humiliating me? I flew all this way!"

And he goes like this, he goes: "Well, gee, Deb—Anthony's my little cousin, you know, and I just had to bring him along to cheer him up, cause he's been so depressed ever since his parents passed away."

Like I don't know there is no cousin Anthony!! Like I don't know the family by heart?

I mean this honeymoon is just the honeymoon from hell, it's just a nightmare…

I mean, he made me wait, I had to wait to get married till after the show, ok? So it's like 12:32 in the morning, Mike's totally exhausted, and there's little Anthony!

I mean so ok, we had to have the ceremony in the suite because of security reasons but he could have had flowers, I mean he could have had romantic music, or something.

I mean, it was so embarrassing there was just…all this stupid Lion King birthday shit, this stupid Lion King shit—I HATE THE STUPID FUCKING LION KING.

And I know he told me sex was out as long as I'm in this condition, I mean it's not like I expected romance and passion on my wedding night, believe me

But I mean, we could have cuddled, we used to cuddle.

I mean, I'm his wife—that's not asking too much…

I said "I'm not gonna bite you, Michael, I love you to death."

It's like he's ashamed of me

I swear, I'm goin' back to the Valley, I'm havin' this baby and then I'm going right back to the life I used to, you know—have, go back to Dr. Klein's, get me a little tract house, with a yard—cause you know what, Mike?

That'll suit me fine.

Dirty Little Secrets

Jeffrey M. Jones

Sherry, a sex-worker, provides details of her long-standing secret relationship with a top presidential advisor. She is speaking, on the record, to a tabloid reporter in exchange for payment, with the understanding that her story will be published and that her name will appear.

SHERRY. So this is by now, we're like maybe a month into it—and I finally go, "I can stay over if you like" and he's like, "Oh, that's great, that's wonderful," so I get there, I'm like knocking—and when he finally gets to the door, he's like "Gee, I musta fallen asleep."

I go, "Hard day at the office, honey?" He goes "Oh, yeah."

He goes, "But you just come over here on the sofa, and lemme make it up to you."

So we start making out and he goes, "Isn't this fun, we're necking like teenagers?"

I'm like…

He goes, "So how we gonna get these pants off, Shari?"

I'm like, "Well Dick, I think you gonna have to take my boots off first…"

He goes, "Oh wow—let me do that—I got a foot fetish, remember?" And he's like sniffing my feet and licking my toes so you know, we do the leg show again,

And then he calls his wife (he calls her Bunny—and they have this whole baby talk thing—I mean it really makes you wanna puke)—

I mean men are really something else.

Here's this guy, one minute he's on the phone to the President of the United States, the next minute he's calling up Bunny, going "booboo gaga."

I'm thinking "What a farce!"

So I finally go, "Does your wife know you're seeing other women?"

He goes, "Oh, well, you know," he goes, "Not exactly—she just says, 'Please, be discrete.' Isn't that wonderful of her?" He goes, "Besides, if I'm not seriously involved, it's not hurting my wife, it's just business."

I go, "Yeah, that's how I feel, too—strictly business."

He goes, "So please don't fall in love with me."

I go, "Don't worry—I won't." And I didn't.

When the time came, I just said, "Bye…"

"See ya…"

DRACULA

Mac Wellman

Lucy, weak from Dracula's blood-letting, revels in speaking unspeakable appetites.

LUCY. Oh, I do feel so thin I barely cast a shadow. Do you know poor Mina throws up everyday? Yes, she does. Every single day. It is quite revolting to be with her on these occasions. One must pretend not to notice. Her weak stomach must have something to do with the lamentable state of poor Jonathan. Quite changed they say he is. Do you suppose he is still capable of love? In the physical, gymnastical sense. Doesn't look it, to be sure. Looks quite the shorn sheep. But I have heard from Simmons, you know Simmons? Jack's man? That the mad are sexually indefatigable. Very goats at it. He described to me quite remarkable feats of copulation among the idiot population of his previous place of employment: Lady Gresham's Home for the Feeble-Minded. It was no point to stop the poor dears. They would, if prevented during sensible hours, get to it, clandestinely, at night. Till the very floors creaked.

The doctors tried straight-waistcoats, but the poor dears would roar and howl so it was more than decency could bear. And, goodness knows, what else would you have them do? The girls were quite clumsy and incapable of acquiring the simplest stitch—I am referring to needlecraft. The men absolute unlicked bears, lost to all possibility of Christian improvement. Simmons kept meticulous records of the more wonderful feats, the most appalling and exuberant lubricities. Simmons calls me *Ishtar* on our little walks over the wold. I make poor old Dr. Van Helsing do that too. He turns red as a beet, but he does it. Do you know he is quite incontinent? He must wear a sort of india-rubber night suit to avoid embarrassment. He calls it an attribute of a certain class of genius. Caesar. Alexander the Great. Willem the Silent. Bedwetters all. That's what dear Van Helsing has told me. I call him "Bobo." Then he pretends to do an examination of me—all because of my dreams, my apparent anemia, and the irritation about my throat.

FIVE FLIGHTS

Adam Bock

Olivia explains the inspiration for her religious aspirations, which includes forming a church honoring the fifth day of creation and the importance of birds.

OLIVIA. Ok.

One day, when I was practicing preaching, outside, it rained. And I thought "We're gonna need a church. With a roof." And a miracle happened. Because that very day, Adele said to me—

My father is dead.

(Long pause.)

Now.

In order to understand why I knew this was a miracle, we have to go back in time.

Imagine:

Two years ago, on the fifth day of my semi-annual fast, which also happened to be on Cinco de Mayo, the fifth of May, which is the fifth month of the year, I was wandering through the basement stacks of the Rochambeau library. Just

I was lightheaded. Well because I was fasting. I was lightheaded. I was discouraged. I had a low-paying job. My car was. My Visa bill was. I felt.

I was in the basement of a library.

So there I was. In the basement. Just reading. Here and there. And I opened a journal. With an article. About a medieval aviary. Not a building aviary. But a book aviary. A medieval book. Written by monks. Which explained everything. In the form of stories about birds.

The vulture devours corpses like a sinner delights in carnal knowledge. And. The sparrow is an inconstant and restless bird. Like a faithless man flying from God. And.

Right. And. Suddenly a flashing insight cut through my lightheadedness and despair.

I realized the bird is God revealing all. On the fifth day of the fifth month of my fortieth year and forty is five times five plus five and five and five, I realized that the fifth day of creation is really the holiest of holy days. Not the sixth, not the seventh, but the fifth. The day God created birds.

And I felt a deep calm. I had a message to share.

FREAKSHOW

Carson Kreitzer

Turn of the previous century. Amalia is perched on a pedestal, against which is propped an old-fashioned, elaborately lettered sign: The Woman With No Arms And No Legs.

AMALIA. You are wondering if I have ever had sexual intercourse. (*Pause.*) Of course. If it has occurred to you already, having only just met me, don't you think it would have occurred to someone before you? Some man some time, who would have found it quite easy to find me alone some night? Of course. Although I have no arms or legs the rest of me is quite normal. My face is even beautiful. I know this. People are not afraid of flattering me or giving me a swelled head, because I have no arms or legs. They don't even say it *to* me, really. I just hear them as they walk by. "MY GOD SHE'S BEAUTIFUL" they say to each other in varied tones of incredulity. How could a freak, they ask themselves, have been blessed with such beauty? That is why people are afraid of me. I have a lover. As a matter of fact. A very sweet man. He is the man who cleans out the animals' cages. His name is Matthew. Good, solid, Biblical name. Ran away to join the circus. Or, more precisely, Mr. Flip's Freakshow and Travelling Jungle. Matthew said he fell in love with me the minute he saw me, but I think he just made that up later. I think he just wanted to get out of that little town. But he is in love with me now. Every night after he is finished shovelling out the elephant shit, he comes to see me. He washes himself thoroughly first. I am the only person who gets to see him clean. He spends all day in the mud. If you were to pass him by when you leave this tent, you would never guess he is my lover. He looks just like any other muddy boy during the day, but ah, you must see him at night. He parts the curtain and tiptoes into the Hall of Freaks. I watch him walking toward me, hair still wet, clean pressed suit, love in his eyes. We are silent so as not to wake the others. Often the Pinhead is awake anyway, singing little songs to himself. Matthew lifts me up and carries me out, back to his bed. Pallet of sweet straw in the wagon. Listening to the animals settling into their sorrow for the night. Sweet good straw and to be off this…DISPLAY for precious moments, held. It's a bit of heaven. A small, manageable bit. Sometimes he takes me for a walk in the woods at night. If the weather is good, sometimes he lays me down and we make love in a field. (*Smiles conspiratorially.*) This is exciting because of the danger. How would he ever explain it if we got caught? It would look pretty bad for him. I would never be blamed—I have no arms or legs. I think the old farmer who discovered us would have a heart attack and die on the spot. Thinking he'd have to chase off a pair of young lovers and instead finding a man and a torso. (*Laughs to herself. After a moment, turns her attention back to the audience.*) You can tell that I am well taken care of. My appearance is neat. I am properly fed. That is all, by the way, because I am beautiful. I've no doubt that if I were born ugly I'd have been thrown in a pit before I was five. But, as I say, I am well taken care of. My hair is brushed. My teeth are brushed. I am washed. I am well taken care of. But there are some days, sitting here silent hour after hour being stared at, when I would gladly commit murder to be able to scratch my nose. Only once have I been taken against my will. The night that Matthew sold me. It's actually not a very interesting story. I'd rather not go into it. Just what you'd think. You can fill in the details. Rich man in some town we passed through got that idea about me, the one we discussed earlier. Asked around, the boys shrugged, said Ask Matthew. Coincidentally, Matthew and I had fought bitterly the night before, about the Pinhead. I had hurt him very badly, so Matthew decided to hurt me back. He came in and warned me first, though. He was crying already. When the Rich Man came and took me, I didn't say a word. Didn't make a sound. I could have been the Mute with No Arms and No Legs for all he knew. (*She finds this amusing.*) In the end, it was much worse for Matthew. He cried at the foot of my pedestal all that night, and for many nights to come. It took me a while to forgive him. That was really a rotten thing to do, after all. I was, uh, very frightened. But I was morally in the right, and Matthew was not. That's why it was worse for him. He learned something about himself, something he didn't want to know. I certainly would never have guessed it was in him. After it happened I knew I shouldn't have been surprised, but I really believed that Matthew was one human being without that astounding capacity for cruelty. I am in love with the Pinhead. That is the tragedy of my life. And perhaps it is also the tragedy of the man who cleans out the animals' cages, but I don't think so. He is still young. As am I, but I seem much older because I have never moved from this spot. Matthew will leave the freakshow, whereas the Pinhead and I will not.

HATE MAIL

Bill Corbett and Kira Obolensky

Dahlia, a struggling photographer, has recently left the city. This form letter reignites a sputtering correspondence with Preston, a neurotic Midwesterner who began their letter exchange with a complaint letter to her former place of employment.

DAHLIA. Greetings from Burlington, Vermont! You may be surprised to get a form letter, but I wanted to celebrate my change of heart and life with *all* of you, my closest friends, but it's hard to write personalized notes to 83 people.

As many of you know, I've had some recent hardships. I lost my job, my health insurance, and my apartment; have had to rethink my entire career as an artist due to an unfortunate collective misinterpretation of my work; and spent three weeks living with an uncle who sniffs adhesives.

Yet all is for the best. That time spent wrapped in a sleeping bag on my uncle's filthy floor was exacted what I needed. I decided to leave New York City!

The change has done me a world of good. I discovered an astonishing collection of like-minded souls here, most of them younger than myself and recently graduated from Hampshire College.

Plus, I've found meaningful work. I'm working with the Coalition Against Pollution, or "CAP"! CAP is very militant, but in a very positive way. We eschew the pretty pictures the Sierra Club and other organizations proliferate to get money. We denounce them as *lies.*

We are raising funds to produce a calendar that will feature the *real* American landscape. Every month will showcase another atrocity committed by capitalism! *(I have learned things about a certain ice cream company that would change forever your feelings about Cookies 'n' Cream.)* The CAP calendar will hang in kitchens across America, a potent reminder of the truth. Yours truly will be the photographer.

Whatever amount you can manage, friends, will go towards graphic design costs, photo developing and the eventual publication of the calendar, which we hope will be carried by a major bookstore chain. (Knock wood!)

I thank you in advance for your generous contribution to this worthy cause.

HISTORY LESSON

David Lindsay-Abaire

Maggie, a park ranger who has been dumped and fired by her boyfriend/boss, gives a (possibly) historically inaccurate tour of Mount Rushmore.

MAGGIE. And what's interesting about George Washington, and most people don't know this about him, he wasn't just the father of our country, he was also the father of the first septuplets born in the United States. Martha gave birth to seven children on October 5th, 1762. Five of the children were very badly behaved, so they were sold into white-slavery, while the two remaining, Maxwell and Hortense, drowned tragically in the Potomac while trying to retrieve their father's wooden teeth, which had fallen out of his mouth while he was beating a seagull with a canoe paddle.

(Beat.)

For those of you just joining the group, my name is Maggie, and today's my last day here at the Mount Rushmore National Memorial. There have been some cutbacks at the National Park Service, so I've been let go, which in my opinion is a huge loss to tourists like yourselves who are hungry for history, because I happen to be what we in the industry call "A font of knowledge."

(Back to the speech.)

Now if you look to the right, you'll notice that the next head belongs to Thomas Jefferson, who, and this may come as a surprise to you, was actually born without skin from the neck down. In fact, he spent most of his childhood in and out of hospitals because of his susceptibility to disease, what with the exposed muscle and sinew and whatnot. But in 1772, his good friend Benjamin Franklin fashioned a crude epidermis out of sheep bladders and carpenter's glue, held together by pewter hooks that Paul Revere forged in his silver shop. Paul Revere, you may have heard, was a Smithy, which is one of my favorite words. He was also a eunuch, which was not very common in the 1700s, though there were a few. I believe Sam Adams was also a eunuch, and...Nathan Hale, who I've been told had a wonderful singing voice. So, that's probably something you haven't heard on any other tour today. It's interesting, isn't it?

(Suddenly.)

Oh, by the way, if any of you happen to have a question, feel free to raise your hand and stick it up your ass.

IN THE WRECKAGE

Matthew Wilson

Amy, a young woman, has a late-night encounter with an unseen person who may or may not actually be there.

AMY. I know you're in there.

Let me in. This isn't funny anymore. Open the door. I'm not kidding. Open the door and let me in.

It's me. You know it's only me.

(*Pause.*)

Can you hear me? I said it's only me. Aren't you listening? Let me in.

I know you're in there.

(*Pause.*)

Oh, isn't this *like* you? Isn't this *just* like you?

We can't stay this way forever, you know. This door is coming open, it's only a question of *when*.

(*Pause.*)

If you open the door we can talk. Would you like that? Would you like to talk?

(*Pause.*)

I would like that. I've been meaning to talk to you. Can we talk?

Can we please talk?

(*Pause.*)

We don't have to talk. Do you want me to stop talking? If I stop talking, will you start? Will you start talking?

(Pause.)

I don't want to stop. I like to talk. No, that's not true. I don't like talking, but I have to. I can't stop it. If you don't start, I can't stop. Do you understand me? Are you listening? I can't stop talking. I have to keep this up so long as I'm out here and you're in there, or, I'm *in* here and you're *out* there or, or, or…*whatever*. But I'll talk so long as the door is closed and you won't come out and you won't start talking and you have to OPEN THE DOOR. DO YOU *HEAR* ME? I SAID *OPEN* IT. *NOW*…

(Pause.)

Did you hear that? My voice? You did that to me. I hope that makes you happy.

It doesn't make me happy.

I said it doesn't make me happy.

I know you're in there.

(Pause.)

What's it like in there? It must be nice. I hope so. I want you to be someplace nice. Is it? Nice and peaceful? It's nice out here. It can be. You don't believe me, but it's true. It can be nice out here. It would be nice if you were here.

(Pause.)

Is it dark? I can't tell. Is it cold? I know it gets cold in there.

I know you're in there.

Come on, come on. A person could go crazy out here. Come on, what's it like? Tell me what it's like. I'm listening. Did you hear me? I said I'm listening. Honest to God, I'm listening this time. Tell me.

(Pause.)

Can I tell you something? Are you listening?

(Pause.)

Remember…remember when I got locked out? Remember that? I drove all the way North because I remembered Cheryl had a key. Remember, and I had to wake her up to get it? She said it was all right, but I could tell she was a little pissed. Only it turned out you were home the whole time. I just didn't know it. I thought you were gone. All I had to do was knock on the door, you would've let me in. Do you remember that? It was so awful. Do you know how awful it was? It was so awful I had extra keys made. Keys to every door, to every room. I've got them here with me. Do you understand? I have a key. I didn't want to do it like this, but I can open the door, I have a key.

(Pause.)

I'm opening the door. Do you hear me? I'm opening it. This is your last chance…

(Pause.)

All right. Ready or not, here I come…

(Pause.)

Oh.

(Pause.)

Oh, well I'll be.

Isn't that my luck? Isn't that *like* you? Isn't that *just* like you?

Not to be there.

IN THE WRECKAGE

Matthew Wilson

Amy, a young woman, has a late-night encounter with an unseen person who may or may not actually be there.

AMY. Little Bastard. I'd say it to his face. I would so. If he was here. I'd say, "You're a real bastard, you bastard. You're a real son of a bitch." That's what I'd say. If he was here.

Probably he'd start laughing. He'd laugh and say, "Oh, come on, I'm not so bad," and I'd say, "Yes, you are, you *are* so bad, you little bastard, you little son of a bitch," and then he'd stop laughing. He'd stop because he would know that I was serious this time. He'd know that because I'd say it to his face. If he was here.

I know what would happen next. He'd be silent a long time. He'd just stare at me while he tried to figure it all out. Then he'd look at me and say, "Now *listen…*," but I wouldn't be listening. Not to him. Not this time. Maybe in the past, but not anymore. I wouldn't have to listen to him anymore. He'd say, "Listen, I won't sit here and have you call me these ridiculous names." I know he would say that. That's the sort of thing he *always* said. Then I'd tell him, "You *will*, you will *absolutely* listen to me. You'll *listen* this time." Oh, it would be so sweet. So sweet to finally say that to him. I'd do it, too. Don't tell me I wouldn't. I'd say it right to his face.

That's when things would really heat up. He'd start screaming now. I'm sure of it. He'd start with the screaming, the accusations… He'd tell me it was all in my head. My imagination. Some nerve. Like he lived inside my head. He doesn't live inside my head. Because that was his way, you know. It was always me. It was never him. It was never his problem. The room was never too cold for him. It had to be too cold for you and could someone please turn up the heat because this other person is freezing to death. Like he could know if I was cold. He doesn't live inside my body and he shouldn't say those things. I wouldn't let him. I'd say, "It's *not* in my head, you bastard. You little son of a bitch. It was *never* in my head, it was always *you*. Stop saying in it was in my head. You don't live inside my head, do you? You don't know *what* goes on there." I'd say that to him. Damn right. He wouldn't know what to do, what to say. He wouldn't know what hit him. I can see it now. Inside my head. Because it *was* him, it *really* was, it was…

Oh, I don't know. I guess I don't know.

No, I *do* know and I'm *right,* and, and, and…IT WAS *HIM.* Little Bastard. That's *exactly* what I would say. If he was here.

Then he would lose it. He'd really lose it. He'd start tearing through the apartment, knocking things over. He'd keep on screaming, but I wouldn't back down. I'd tell him to take a hike. I'd tell him he was a leech, that he sucked the life right out of people, I'd tell him the whole world didn't revolve around him and his problems and I'd say it to his face. I'd look him right in the eye and tell him to quit sucking the rest of the world down in his little sinkhole. He'd yell and scream and throw things around the room and I'd stand my ground. I wouldn't give in no matter what and he'd go nuts and he'd put his fist through the window again and it would really be something.

Wouldn't it? Wouldn't that be something? That would really be something.

If he was here.

INVISIBLE WOMAN

Rich Orloff

Susanne has just been asked by the man she's dating how she is. Although she assures him nothing is happening in her life, her unspoken answer is far more complex.

SUSANNE.
You want to know how I am? Well, that makes two of us.
You want to know the thoughts in my head?
Well, so do I.
At least, part of me does.
And part of me doesn't.
And the part of me that doesn't, rules.
Mostly I keep busy, so I won't have
time to listen to myself.
I keep busy, because I'm afraid
if I take time, there may be
nothing to listen to.
And every now and then,
when I do hear something,
I get scared.
What does that thought mean?
What am I supposed to do with it?
Where should I put it?
When it goes away, I breathe easier;
And I try to get busy again.
Other people, I look at them, and
They seem so filled with
thoughts and feelings.
How can they get any work done?
If I felt and thought as much as
most people, I don't think I'd have

the energy for anything else.
Sometimes I think feeling and thinking
is a fad, and one day it'll pass.
Somewhere,
Somewhere inside me,
I know I must have that which others have;
And if I forced myself,
I could feel all that's inside.
I'm sure if I forced myself,
If I really forced myself,
And I got over the urge to scream,
I could tell you a great deal.
But what if I couldn't stop?
And what if I stayed that way,
Thinking and feeling all over the place,
Every waking moment?
And telling you all about it;
Getting so that I wanted to;
And that I needed someone to listen?
No, that doesn't sound the least bit attractive.
And if I told you everything I thought
And everything I felt
And everything I desired,
And when I finished,
If, but for a split second,
You looked at me in silence,
I'd feel so alone
That the terror would collapse my heart.
And even if I survived that,
Even if I survived the terror,
You'd know where my soul lived;
And I need to have an unlisted soul.
I know you seem to like me,
But I know you don't know me.
So what does your affection mean?
And I see that you're kind.
And I see you try to bring me out.

But I don't trust it's what you really want.
No, even if I knew what I thought and felt,
I could not tell you.
So please stop asking.
I could love you if you stopped asking.
Please.
Please
Order your drink,
And let's have dinner,
And tell me stories of your day
And of your life.
Distract me, engage me,
Let me live through you.
You can do that, I know you can.
It's your most attractive feature.
Just stop asking me how I am,
Please,
Before I get annoyed,
Before I lose patience,
And get so fed up I tell you,
And risk it all,
And face the terror I have not yet
named but which runs my life.
And if you make me go there,
I will only resist you
And resent you,
And neither of us will be happy.
So you tell me how you are,
And I will listen,
And I will take your hand,
And I'll make you glad you're a man.
But I will not tell you how I am.
I cannot tell you.
Ever.

Iphigenia in Tauris

translated by Edward Seymour
from the play by Johann Wolfgang von Goethe

After rejecting King Thoas's advances for high-minded reasons, Iphigenia is forced to deceive him in order to free the two Greek prisoners, whose true identity she has discovered. The King's unconscious assumption of male superiority enrages her.

IPHIGENIA. *(After some moments' silence:)*
Are men alone entitled to perform
Great ventures, then? Are they alone required
To grapple with impossibility?
The deeds that men call great, that lift the spirits
Each time their story is repeated, did
They not begin in courage, when success
Looked most unlikely? Those who single-handed
Outwit the enemy, at dead of night
Appear among them like a raging fire,
Fall on the drowsy, startled men until,
Hard pressed by those they've roused, they gallop back
On stolen horses with their plunder, are they then
Alone deserving of our praise? Or those
Who spurn the easy road and boldly cross
Mountain and forest country, with the aim
Of clearing all the land around of bandits?
Is nothing left for us? Must a gentle woman
Forsake her native right to gentleness,
Be brutal with the brutes, like Amazons
Plunder your right to violence, and avenge
With blood our long oppression? Bold endeavour
Rises and falls within my beating heart:
I can expect fierce condemnation and

Great evil if I fail in my attempt;
I place the outcome in your lap alone!
If you are true, as you are said to be,
Then prove it by supporting me, and give
Glory through me to truth! —The truth, O King,
Is yes, a secret plot is being forged:
You ask in vain to see the prisoners;
They have gone, and they are fetching their companions
Who wait on board the ship down at the coast.
The older man, seized by an evil here
Which has now left him—he is Orestes,
My brother, and the other one his friend
And confidant from boyhood days, Pylades.
Apollo sent them here from Delphi with
A holy mission to remove Diana's
Image and bring the sister to him, which
He promised to reward by freeing him
From Furies and the guilt of matricide.
I have now put us both, the last survivors
Of Tantalus's house, within your hands.
Destroy us—if you can.

I THINK YOU THINK I LOVE YOU

Kelly Younger

Branwyn, a comically high-strung woman, has just returned from spreading her mother's ashes. She had to do it alone because, as she explains to her date here, of a damn cat.

BRANWYN. That's it. This feral cat that lives in the parking lot where her office is. She starts feeding this thing, and of course she has to name it and names it Henry, so she starts feeding this thing two, three times a day for about three years. But then when she gets transferred across town, she still goes back to feed it. Two, three times a day. Can you believe that? To leave on your lunch break and go feed a feral cat named Henry at your old job where they transferred you in the first place to get rid of you? And you keep coming back because Henry will supposedly starve to death if she doesn't feed it? And she does this for like another five years, sometimes even getting my mother to go do it when she had a meeting or something if you can believe it, until finally she decided to trap it in a cage. Then she brings Henry home to her apartment, which already has four cats living there—she's one of those women, you know? With a lot of cats?—but Henry of course flips out and the other cats flip out because he's feral and they're not, but then they start acting feral and peeing all over her carpet because they're mad that Lauren brought home this stray. And she has to keep Henry living in a cage, in her kitchen. She never lets the thing out? And she sees nothing wrong with this. So the whole apartment now stinks of cat urine but she thinks this is all in my head and that I'm criticizing her, which of course I am. Wouldn't you?

I THINK YOU THINK I LOVE YOU

Kelly Younger

Branwyn, a comically high-strung woman, should be making small talk while on a date, but instead can't stop talking about her mother's recent death.

BRANWYN. I know, I know. I'm just kidding. Like I said, I'm in a mood, you know? But it's what she wanted. Not to die, of course, but to hike. Once it got her. Leukemia. That's what it ended up being, even though it didn't start out that way. I mean it did, of course. The doctor said leukemia first, and we we're all like—oh my God!—and she went through all this chemo, you know, a whole summer of it. And then the doctor couldn't find any trace of it. The leukemia. And we all started thinking, maybe she never had it to begin with, you know? Maybe they couldn't find any *(Using her fingers to make quotation marks:)* "trace of it" because it was maybe never there. That happens sometimes, you know, where they misdiagnose and of course there's no *(Using her fingers:)* "trace of it" …God, I swore I'd never be that annoying person who uses her hands to make *(Using her fingers:)* "bunny ears." But once we thought she maybe never had it, she up and dies. And after we had the bone marrow test and of course the only match is my sister who turned the whole thing into some conspiracy against her, you know, like of course *she* would be a match and I wouldn't because mom and I we're always a better match and now the one time they get along it's because mom wants to suck the marrow out of her bones—literally, you know—and by the time I convinced her to go through with it she was of course relieved to find out she didn't have to do it, but then it turned out she *did* in fact have traces of it, it was just hiding. And of course it came out of hiding so quickly that it just jumped out and said, *(Using her fingers:)* "I'm back, I'm moving in, bought, sold and furnished, home sweet home" in my mother's body and then that was that.

JIMMY CARTER WAS A DEMOCRAT

Rinne Groff

Emily is a fierce union organizer for air traffic controllers. She despises grav-ity—how it teaches for every flight of success, there is always a fall.

EMILY. There's a lot of pressure, a lot of pressures, a lot of forces that conspire to keep us down.

Gravity is the worst, of all those forces. You can't get away from it. Gravity's always there. It dooms us straight from the start. I read somewhere that when a woman gets pregnant, you know egg and sperm, right away that little package starts turning and stuff, and it's all affected by gravity. I mean, even before we know who we are, even before we're born; this shit, it's just pulling on us. It colors everything. What's the first thing that pops into your head when you hear these words: Up? High? She's flying? Those ought to be nice words, great words, words of potential. But on account of gravity, all you can think of is the inevitable Down; Low; She's crashed.

But then there's airplanes, right? And you watch them and you think they've really got it figured out. When a plane's taking off and there it goes gliding upwards, or if you're riding in one of those new jets, so smooth, if you have a good pilot, you could maybe forget about your morbid visions of tailpipes in flames and really believe, believe for a moment that you can overcome... fuck, you could overcome anything, you're flying, you did it.

Why can't that be the way we think? Why can't we teach our chil-dren that in the womb? Not to be afraid. Not to assume yeah, sure you're Up now, but here comes Failure, you might as well throw in the towel. And if a baby could feel all right, up in the air, in a plane, soaring along, could experience freedom from all that pulls her down; if she could learn that, can't you maybe imagine that she could get free of a bunch of other shit, too? That we'd grow as a species and triumph? And change, and growth, and all that are possible?

She's flying. She's flying.

THE JOYS OF CHILDHOOD

Kirsten Greenidge

Claudette Cox, an overzealous and overprotective mother, is interviewing for a new nanny after the last one had to be let go. She gives a list of detailed instructions pertaining to the care of her daughter.

CLAUDETTE COX. *(Sits cross-legged with pen and clipboard:)* So. *(Smiles.)* Let's see here. *(Regards clipboard:)* Vassar: wonderful. I'm a Yalie, myself. Study abroad: fan*tas*tic. Although I see here you spent your time in Paris and the children study Spanish—personally I'm with you: *viva* la *France*—but maybe you could take a class? Or listen to one of those tapes, one of those language tapes. Yes? Now, the position isn't terribly difficult. School ends at three, violin on Mondays, ballet Tuesdays and Thursdays, pottery every other Wednesday, calligraphy every other *other* Wednesday and riding every Friday. *(Pause.)* No. No, no it's not too much activity: they're *bright*; they're *exceptionally* bright. Now where was…oh, yes, Riding-on-Fridays. Except every third Friday when Sequoia—my oldest and the one with *the (Motions around her eyes with her pinky finger, then whispers)* …patch: yes. We don't talk about that. *(Zips her mouth shut.)* Every third Friday Sequoia visits Woody. Woody is our code name for Dr. Green. Dr. Green-the-therapist. Even though Sequoia's down to once a month we don't talk about Woody, either. *(She motions around her eyes, and then her ear in a circle with her pinky finger, then makes a slicing motion with her hand in the air.)* Which brings me to my next point: we have several rules we follow for Sequoia. Woody / Dr. Green-the-therapist suggested them and they seem to, um, keep her calm. *(Smiles uneasily and consults her clipboard:)* First, when preparing food: use spices that are white. Nothing green, nothing black and under no circumstances *ever:* red. She says spices look like eyes staring at her and Dr. Woody, I mean, Woody/Dr. Green-the-therapist explained we should treat her fears with understanding.

Eyes: what a robust imagination: we may have an artist on our hands, I'm telling you. Now: two: when the girls are home we… *(Smiles.)* we cover the floors—well, anywhere Sequoia needs to walk—with towels. I keep the linen closet stocked so you shouldn't run out: Sequoia has developed an aversion to our wall-to-wall. She says the bristles are like spears. Little spears piercing the soles of her feet. As you can understand we can't let her feel like that so— … No, she can*not* *"just* wear *shoes"*: no, no, no, no, no. Woody explained that would be insensitive, monstrous even. Imagine clipping a bird's wings or chopping a gazelle's legs off at the knees so it's forced to leap around with bloody stumps instead of legs. Woody says Sequoia's preferences are part of her nature, her very being. So we lay down towels and she gets around the house perfectly fine that way. And make sure you line each hallway: we don't want her stuck in a room somewhere. Third, when serving snacks and dinner *don't* use the cobalt blue plates. Or the glasses, or the bowls: any of the dishware, really. Apparently she can taste the glass; she says it rubs off onto her food. One night one of the nannies forced her to eat off those glass plates and she began choking. Shards of glass were tearing her throat, she said, the blue from the cobalt glasses was staining her teeth and tongue, poisoning her, she said. She got so upset we let her have desert without finishing first. I scraped the foil off those Hershey's kisses myself—she hates the foil-feel, you'll want to remember. She calmed right down which is… *(Touches her nose with her pinky.) exactly:* what Woody thinks is best: yes, *yes*. I *like* you. I'm confident you'll fit in beautifully. Not like that other nanny; that glass wielding nazi-nanny. The night she tried to kill my Sequoia, she said that she thinks Sequoia is making all this up, that she's pulling our legs, that while I was removing the wrapping off of Sequoia's prematurely presented sweet snack Sequoia winked at her. Winked? How preposterous. Sequoia is a *gazelle*. We are to help her *Leap*, Woody explained. Winked: can you believe that? Honestly: I'm glad we got rid of *her*. Now, when can *you* start?

LAST LOVE

Peter Papadopoulos

On the eve of their five-year wedding anniversary, Lucida confronts her husband after finding that he has once again left the toilet seat up. When he admits that he has being doing it intentionally, she chastises him for the many ways he has failed their relationship.

LUCIDA.
How careless you have become!
With me. With our love.

In the beginning
there were flowers
my favorites
alstroemeria
and roses
and sometimes even black-eyed susans
and there were invitations to meet you for dinner
at my favorite restaurants
Veritas
and Sals
and Dominics
and there were phone calls
down the hall to my office
and later
over to McCutcheon and Smith's
to ask how my day was going
at my new job
and can I bring you, perhaps, a sandwich
if you don't have time for lunch
and even surprise visits
and sometimes the closing of doors and blinds
and a quick and passionate romance on my desk

with pencils digging into my behind
and then
leaving me with a rose
which you had thought to buy on the way over.

And now…
now it's the leaving of the toilet seat up
and NOT EVEN in a careless way
because you said you do it intentionally.
And I think
it's alright that the flowers have long since disappeared
one expects this
and the calls to go out to dinner
have become infrequent
and the quickies at the office have totally evaporated.
Like your career.
This is to be expected after a few years,
when the heat has died down,
but leaving the toilet seat up—
something so small and ridiculous
now done intentionally
defiantly
a premeditated act of disrespect.

THE LAST ORBIT OF BILLY MARS

Robert Alexander

Mama, a bed-ridden mother to the universe of all children she comes in contact with, is asking Billy Mars to be patient in his pursuit of her daughter Rita Mae. Rita Mae is bi-sexual and may be incapable of giving Billy everything he is seeking in a relationship with her.

MAMA. Rita Mae might be incapable of giving you everything you want. I mean—I used to go to bed at night and try to imagine what her big day would be like. I'd try to imagine how she'd look coming down the aisle of the church she grew up in, wearing the same wedding gown I wore. As hard as I tried—I kept turning up nothing. Well, one day I was up there in the attic cleaning it out—Rita Mae was helping me. So I got her to try on my wedding dress. She was 'bout the same size I was the day I got married…built a lot like me. She put on the dress and it fit her to a T. Yet, something was missing. That glow—a woman gets—from putting on a special dress—was missing from her face. It was then that she told me she was gay. I cried, "Lawd—tell me it ain't so—tell me it ain't so." Rita Mae said, "I'm sorry, Mama." I said, "What you got to be sorry about? God is the one who should be sorry. He's the one who made you that way." It was that day that I realized that I could no longer dream my children's dreams for them. They came here with dreams of their own. And I had stop trying to force my dreams onto them. Marrying Rita Mae is your dream. But your dream and her dream might not be the same. Will you still love her if she says no?

THE LAST ORBIT OF BILLY MARS

Robert Alexander

Rita Mae, a vulnerable child-like woman in her 30s is talking to her mother and brother, remembering what it was like driving along in heavy freeway traffic in LA and connecting it to the memory of growing up next to a highway in St. Louis. She is not playing with a full deck.

RITA MAE. Growing up so close to the freeway—I was programmed for freeway living. See—when you got a freeway for a front yard—there's no sense of community…I mean—you can't cross the street and say hello to your neighbor. You can't wave or talk idly about the weather or compliment him on the roses in his rose garden. You can't talk—say hello to the mailman without shouting, your voice trailing off with the traffic blowing by. If someone says something you didn't quite hear, you smile politely, pretend you heard it, and change the subject to something else. L.A. was a place to go if you a had a fear of intimacy…a fear of getting to know your neighbor—marking time alone in your car, sitting on the freeway, breathing in the fumes of civilization. You turn off your air conditioner, roll down your window. Suddenly— you don't feel so cut off. And so you start to sing a little tune to yourself at first, but then you start singing louder and louder to anyone and everyone. So what if you only know half the words and can't decide what key you're in. You're just glad to be alive and be in L.A. in the middle of this mass of humanity and machinery clogging up the freeway. And so you sing. You sing and sing, until the little white men in little white coats come and take you away—or you sing until the traffic starts to move—whichever happens first.

THE LAST WOMAN ON EARTH

Liz Duffy Adams

It's the year 2509, exactly ten minutes before the end of the world, and the 512-year-old (though still apparently young) title character is declining to board the last evacuation ship. As the clock ticks, she tells its captain and her Lunatic (moon-born) assistant why.

EARTHLING. Fuck yes, I'm tired, I'm fucking whacked but that's not it, that's not my POINT, it's memories, Christ's sake, I'm FULL. Every word you say is lodging itself into a FULL HOUSE. Not a question of good memories, bad memories, acres and acres of ordinary memories, I'm full, it's too much, I don't want any more. From the moment my dad woke me up one midnight and said, look, honey, it's the new millennium, you'll always remember this. And now he's been dead four hundred and forty years and I'm a walking graveyard of memory. I'm the only living human to remember graveyards, or automobiles or cassette players or who the Beatles were. I remember phone numbers and street addresses when there are no longer phones or streets. I remember a sway-backed horse in a muddy field, a flock of tiny black birds over a marsh, burning cold feet in ice-skates as twilight fell. I remember the crash of two thousand and one, the Accidental Armageddon of '23, the great biodiversity crisis of the mid-twenty-first. I can still smell the acrid smoke of the fall of New York. I have a scar on my back from the mutant riots of twenty-three-thirty and a lingering glow in my heart from the first wave of the Re-enlightenment. I remember the great gleaming space-liners taking off full of emigrants when the New Colonial Period began, the piercing cries of seagulls after the roar of engines died away and the emptiness of the streets afterwards. And I remember everyone I ever fucked and every one I loved, I remember endless snatches of then crucially bitter or joyful conversations, I remember embarrassing moments from centuries ago—natch—I know the lyrics of a billion idiot pop songs, the plots of millions of novels and movies and sense-o-sa-gas, I know a thousand-year-old children's game. Ashes, ashes, but I don't fall down. *(To* Lunatic:*)* How long?

THE LESSONS OF MY FATHER

Catherine Filloux

Odile, a French-Algerian woman, vividly recollects her just-deceased father, through the eyes of her childhood self. How can you go on breathing when the man who taught you how is gone?

ODILE. To start is, never to end... Along the roads of Oran are the telephone poles your own father installed. Who uses the phones now? Your mother a seamstress, takes you a little boy to the factory, sets you on the table, the seamstresses play with you, teach you to love women. You bring me home tadpoles and a baby stork. At the harbor you look for what is cheap to make us laugh. Your brother flying across the Mediterranean, killed in a fog crash, plane goes down. From that day—the day you and I go to identify his body—you never shave your beard or moustache. Until today when they shave it for you because you are dead.

Every piece of history dies, the smoke of the cigarillos you used to smoke, which made your moustache yellow, your laugh, the revolver you kept in your night table, your daughter, they will lower the lid of the coffin and I will never. Never see... See... Never see you...

LISTENERS

Jane Martin

Eleanor, discovering that the leader of her country is listening to her conversations, speaks freely for the first (and last) time.

ELEANOR. Sir? It's me, Citizen Leftwich.

I mean, I'm nobody in particular, just a dental technician, sidelining in a little discreet hair removal, but I guess if…well, if you're really listening…

I guess I'd really like to say…

Well, I'm kind of getting the feeling…

…that you've fucked us all.

You've butchered our youth for dreams of empire, squandered our children's patrimony, enriched at untold social cost the inconceivably rich, battered our economy, ballooned our deficit, fractured our safety nets, demeaned the values that gave us pride in a national identity, fattened our cynicism…

…endangered our public education, made quislings of our librarians, dismantled our privacy, manipulated our fears, detained and tortured and bombed and killed men and women and children, appalled the world…

…and all, all, all out of some blind, groping, self-serving, economic, geopolitical, theocratic impulse, untouched by real thought or empathy, at the behest of the entitled and corporate…

…that can only end in the poisoning, beyond imagination, of our humanity and our poor earth, you stupid, boorish, vulgar, avaricious, heartless, shallow, incomprehensible, smug, smarmy, illiterate prick!!

LIVES OF THE GREAT WAITRESSES

Nina Shengold

Kay, a born-again waitress in her 40s, explains what it takes to be one of the greats. The role was originally played by an actress of color.

KAY. You either got it, or you don't. If you don't, you won't ever. So don't even bother. Don't strain. Oh, there's things you can learn, sure. The fine points. The stance. "Heat that up for you?" "Toasted?" But honey—scratch that, make it hon—a truly great waitress is *born*.

You get what I mean? It's a feel thing. Deep under the bones of your bones. In your cells. Some reporter once asked Louis Armstrong what "swing" meant. Louis looked the guy dead in the eyeball and said, "If you gotta ask, you'll never know." *He* would've made a great waitress.

My very first diner, we had one. Flo Kelly. A goddess in Supp-hose. Flo was all waitress. She could fill two dozen shakers one-handed and never spill one grain of salt. She could carry eight Hungry Man specials lined up on her arm like a charm bracelet. Flo could serve pie a la mode so it looked like Mount Everest topping the clouds. She poured gravy like tropical rain. In Flo's maraschino-nailed fingers, the short-order carousel spun like the Wheel of Fortune, and never, not once, did a customer's coffee get cold.

Well, I mean to tell you, that diner was *hers*. If Jesus Himself Amen came in and sat down to supper, he would've tipped double. Then one Blue-Plate Special, right after the lunch rush, Flo hung up her hairnet, cashed in her checks and went sunnyside up. And that's when the Lord took my order. I knew what I was. I was called.

(She steps closer.)

Look in my eyes. I know mysteries way beyond menus. I have felt the Lord's love pierce my heart like a skewer through gyros. I have seen Jesus weep ice-kold milk with a K.

(She holds out her hand.)

Heat that up for you? Hon?

LIVES OF THE GREAT WAITRESSES

Nina Shengold

Tammie Sue is a dithery waitress in her 30s with a slight Southern twang. She refills sugar shakers as she speaks.

TAMMIE SUE. So this fella sits down at my counter. Scrawny, beat, banty thing, ugly as yesterday's home fries, and he's got the look. You all know that look.

(She demonstrates.)

There's this puppy dog whimpering back of his eyes, means he's looking for more than two eggs on a raft, wreck 'em, cuppa joe light. So I do what a girl's gotta do. I ignore him. No warm-ups, no sass, save my smile for the grandpas and wedding rings in the next booth. Comes the end of my shift, and this shriveled-up walnut, this cottage cheese curd, this crust of burnt toast is still sitting there. Dog in his eyes rolls right over and begs.

So I give him the deep-freeze. I shoot him a look that would flatten meringue.

(She demonstrates.)

And what's he do? Smiles at me. *Smiles.* Gatty teeth, great big space in the middle, looked just like a little ole kid with skinned knees on the playground.

Well, hell. That did melt me up. Kay's always telling me I got a heart as big as a Butterball turkey, and besides it's been way, way too long since my griddle got greased. So we go to the motor home up top his semi.

Well. I tell you that man had a mouth that could melt you like butter and syrup on top of a short stack of buckwheats. He did things with his fingers that should be illegal, or fattening. That little runt had him a secret self under his outfit.

We've all of us got one, but this was a secret worth spreading around. And he did. He most certainly did. He could love you up one side and back down the other and still leave the middle part gasping for more. That man had a gift. Mashed potatoes and gravy. I left him a tip, that's the God's honest truth.

So the next time you find yourself checking out someone's dessert case, remember, it isn't the Dream Whip that counts. It's the peach in the pie.

LIVES OF THE GREAT WAITRESSES

Nina Shengold

Melissa, an aspiring actress, just finished a hard first day at a waitress job, training under a disapproving supervisor who wants her fired.

MELISSA. This is my first day of work. Not here. Ever. My family had money and nobody made me. I came to this city to look for a job and nobody would hire me. It's kind of like being a virgin—I'm not any more, but I was once, you know?—and I'm telling you, nobody wants to be first. Too much pressure. My roommate said, "Lie." So I did.

People think if you haven't done something before, you're an idiot. People can't know what's inside you. You don't know yourself till you're given a chance. Then all of a sudden this new personality starts to swell under your skin, bursting through where you'd never expect it, and nothing you thought you were makes any sense. You're elastic. You're putty. You've been up for hours, making love to a man whose back ripples with muscles you've never felt, feeling your body expand and explode and dissolve into air, into something like stars, and it doesn't seem possible that you could open your eyes to the same old alarm clock and fit in the same pair of shoes.

I don't want to lose this. This newness, this urgent, sharp knowledge that everything matters. That being good matters.

I want to do everything well.

I know, I'm a waitress. It's not what I've dreamed of, what anyone dreams of, but I make a difference. I do. There are lives on each stool at that counter. The old man who's ordered his Sanka and shredded wheat every morning for twenty-five years.

(She nods towards someone in the audience.)

Otto.

The woman who fought with her husband last night and treated herself to French toast with her friend who just had a mastectomy. Velma and Ruth.

The man who panhandled the price of his coffee. Muhammed.

I touch them. I give them the quiet sensation that once in their sad, uncontrollable lives, they wanted a small thing and got it. I brought it. I bore them a gift. And that matters.

You watch me. I'm going to be brilliant. I'm going to be one of the greats.

THE LUNCH DATE

Garth Wingfield

Holly has just been left by her long-time boyfriend, Matthew. She's also just begun a new adventure that involves wine at lunch, red meat...and a woman she met in group therapy.

HOLLY. So she shows up—looking amazing, I might add. And we sit down and have a couple of glasses of wine—I know, in the middle of the day, totally decadent. And as we're eating our salads—Caesar for me, mixed greens for her; not sure why I just told you that—she just... she puts her hand on my knee. Under the table. And I positively... I swoon. I do! Right there in Montrachet.

And I also just... *know*. In that moment, it becomes very clear. *This is it*, Julia and me, the two of us until we grow old. My heart is fluttering, and I don't know when I've been happier... I don't know when I've ever felt more alive, more... *right* with everything.

And that's when it hit me: I'm a lesbian! This is who I am now. Hold on, and *if* I'm a lesbian, then just... fuck it.

(Fast:)

I cancel the tuna steak and order the t-bone.

I did! With french fries and slaw. And red wine. And lots of bread. Now that I've got the waiter's attention, I pre-order a chocolate mousse for dessert.

I mean, if I'm gonna be a lesbian, then the world can kiss my fat ass—I'm gonna be a beer-bellied, big-tittied BULL DYKE!

I'm gonna eat red meat. I'm gonna deep-tongue kiss girls in public.

I'm gonna bare my titties in the Gay Pride Parade!

I'm gonna be a dyke on a bike and wear leather in *late June* even though it's blistering hot and leather tends to chafe!

And I'm having these thoughts, and Julia's wiping this trickle of blood from my steak off my chin, and before I even know it, I sort of… I manage to brush my hand along her breast… very casually…

(Then:)

Let's face it, I grabbed her tit. I grabbed her tit with this stunning sense of entitlement. Right there in Montrachet.

And Julia gasps, and I gasp, and everyone sees it. What have I done? I've touched this woman in public. I've done this thing. This shocking thing! There's this palpable silence all around…

And I just… start to cry. I can't help it, the tears just come.

(She's crying now.)

I miss Matthew. I miss him so much.

This isn't me. What am I even doing here?

My God, what was I thinking, *going on a date with a woman?*

(HOLLY pulls herself together a bit, tries to stop crying. As she sniffles:)

I mean, come on… I can't eat red meat. It makes my stomach all upset.

And Julia is a lipstick lesbian. She's not gonna want to date some bull dyke.

And the worst part is… I'm gonna see her on Thursday! In group? If Julia brings this up, I'll absolutely die.

I don't believe I just told you all this!

MALL SANTA SAVES THE DAY

Don Zolidis

Julia is a female mall Santa and is explaining the true meaning of a materialistic Christmas to her naive co-worker.

JULIA. You see, you've lost sight of something Bob. Something really important. And it's not something you can buy, and it's not worth money. It's Christmas Spirit.

And Christmas Spirit is what compels people to smile at their neighbors around this time of the year, and it nudges them into their cars even when it's cold outside, and it gently pushes them toward large shopping centers, and even though they can't afford presents because they've been laid off, they still spend exorbitant amounts of money on presents for their inconsiderate children who will forget about it all a few days later. And maybe, just maybe, two of those parents out there are divorced, and maybe they think that if they spend just a bit more money this holiday season, they can buy love from their messed up child who resents them both. And that's what Christmas is about.

Buying love. So you just remember that when you get all uppity with your peace on earth and goodwill towards man.

MEDEA

Joseph Goodrich

Medea's husband, Jason, has left her for the King's daughter. After threatening the lives of the King and his daughter, Medea has been exiled to another country. Jason promises that everything will be taken care of when she's gone and claims to still feel love for her, but after all Medea's sacrificed for her husband, she has little faith in what he has to say.

MEDEA. After what you've done
You have the gall to show up here
And say all that to me?
You hypocrite.
You fucking hypocrite.
You spit in my face and tell me
I'm beautiful?
You murder our love, then offer
To pay for the funeral?
Is that the way an honorable man behaves?
I'm glad you're here, though, in a way.
It gives me the chance to make you hear
The truth.
You've heard of it, the truth? It's like a
Woman's love: Undeniable, absolute, durable
As iron but shattered by a single lie.

When you were looking for the golden fleece,
Who killed the serpent wrapped around
The treasure? Anyone on board the Argo
At the time will tell you it was me.

Who wrapped himself in glory
When the fleece was found?

That was you.

Who murdered Pelias, who butchered
The old king and made sure his
Daughters got the blame?

Who left the home she loved,
Who tore apart her family,
Who threw her past away
In the madness of a moment?
Who has blood on her hands
And on her conscience?

Me.

Medea did.

Medea has.

Who was all this done for?
Who was I trying to please?
One man, and one man only:

You.
You, Jason.
Jason.
Jason.
Jason.
Jason.
Only you.

Whose love justified the butchery,
The damage and destruction?

Yours.

Your love...for me.

MEDEA

Joseph Goodrich

Medea's husband, Jason, has left her to marry the King's daughter for the love of money. Out of spite, Medea has killed their children. Medea then justifies her actions to Jason.

MEDEA. Zeus knows what I've done for you and
How you treated me. Say what you want.
He knows the truth. You can't love me
One day and throw me away the next.
You can't have me exiled just because
I'm inconvenient to your plans. You
Don't break vows when you get tired
Of keeping them. Jason, you can't do
That and get away with it.
Not with me.

You call me a savage, a heathen, an animal.
You say I'm evil. Of course I am; I have to
Be—it's so much easier on the conscience
To know you're saving the world and not
Just acting in your own self-interest.
Tell me—who's the real savage?…Call
Me anything you like if it makes you happy.
What does it matter when I've got what I
Want: Your heart on a stick.

MOTHER RUSSIA

Jeffrey Hatcher

In post-Soviet Moscow, an ancient White Russian recalls the circumstances of her family's flight from the 1917 revolution.

PRINCESS. It confused them too. That is what saved us. They thought we were here, in Moscow, but we were not. We were at...home. *(Weepy, gains force.)* You cannot imagine the life we lost. On a summer's morning, the servants would wake the family at dawn, and the whole house would start off across the fields to the woods until it came at last to a clearing in the deep of the pine forest. Before noon there would be mushroom picking; afterwards a rug was spread in the shade of the birch trees. The samovar whistled. The sun shone. And as the men and women drank yellow wine from green glasses there would be music from balalaikas and the youngest child would recite Pushkin from memory. After that, the day would end, and the family would make its way back through the forest, down the birch avenue until it caught sight of the estate church where lived the priest, the serfs, and Pronka the Fool! And then home, to Vallashevko, where a ball would be held that night. And as the sky turned purple, pedestals were set amid the garden, pedestals that supported statues that were in fact not statues, that were in fact nude peasants papa paid to pose in the garden, their bodies painted white with cream, motionless, as we danced under the lanterns and the stars. Motionless...until the day they came down from their pedestals to crush our skulls.

MOTHER RUSSIA

Jeffrey Hatcher

A reformed prostitute tells a Russian witch how she met her husband, a minister who saved her from a life on the streets by paying her not to have sex.

TATTY. *(Eager and relieved:)* Thanks.

(She takes a cigarette and inhales a long drag. Her body relaxes. Her eyes close. She leans back and starts to talk.)

(Puffs away.)

I became a lady of the evening. A prostitute. A hooker. I worked the subway, the bus station, 42nd Street between eighth and ninth before it became a fuckin' DisneyLand. I had a pimp, his name was Sloop Dinger, and The Dinger was cool, he only wailed on me when he was really crazed on crystal meth, but I didn't feel it 'cause, shit, I was fucked on meth myself, but anyway he got whacked by some Iranian freak he burned on some highly questionable snuff film he ripped off from some Mexican, and I hadda go free-lance, which was not fun in winter, so I hooked up with this chick who was running tail outta her brownstone on East 53rd street. Her real name was, like, Muffeletta Pizzerferonto, and she went by "Inez," but we called her "Joan Crawford," and she got me off the meth, fixed my teeth, put me on diet pills, she was like a mother, man, she put me together with some nice guys, I mean, return business, brand name, not bar rail. But then she had to go and put the moves on me, which I didn't mind, I can Hoover the rug as much as the next vacuum. But she got really freaky and possessive, and then one night she caught me in the sweat house with some righteously bountiful African pussy named Wakeesha, and she went ape and tried to cut me, so I cracked her over the head with a Cuervo bottle, took her credit cards, and me and Wakeesha had some poon-tang time in Bimini for three weeks until the local federales incarcerated us for ten days on some trumped-up charge, so we bided our time turning tricks in stir, which was o.k. for a while, I mean, I'm up for anything, but "daylight come and I wanna go home." So who shows up but Sister Agnes Moorehead, who says, "You, ma-belle, can come home, but Jerk Chicken here stays on island time." So I burned Wakeesha, who seemed glad to be rid of me, frankly, and I moved back in with Mommie Dearest, but things weren't the same, so I said, "Look, I don't wanna be Mrs. Alice B. Stein anymore," and she said, "Fine, I was gonna throw you out on your Mile High Ass anyway." So I moved to a fleabag off 9th Avenue, started free-basing, only work I could get was at this sleazy hotel bar where the ye olde publican would let me troll for marlin in exchange for a quick zip in the men's room. Then one night, I'm workin' the bar at the Milford Plaza, it's summer, it's hot, the Fleet's in, and that's never good news...when this guy suddenly appears at my elbow. And he's wearin' the black suit and the reverso collar and he's carrying a Bible. And he says, "Jesus loves you." And I say: "Great, tell Jesus it costs fifty bucks." And he says, "No, Jesus loves your soul. Jesus doesn't want your body. Jesus wants what you have inside if you'll let him in." Well, this is off the vine, but I say, "Listen, John-Boy, be you Christ or be your Cracker, the price is fitty buck, now lay out to lay me or lam." So he hands me a fifty, and he says, "I will give you fifty dollars not to have sex with me." Which is incredible, it's like paying a farmer not to plant corn, but I take it, and I tell him, you bought yourself an hour, the clock's runnin'. So he sticks out his arm—he's like the guy from a box of chocolates—and I slip off the stool and we walk, and we talk about me and my goddamn soul. And Jesus. And God. And we walk some more. Uptown, downtown, east, west. And the hour goes, and we click the meter, but I don't ask for more money, and it's not hot anymore, it's cool, and the air is sweet, and there are stars and smiles and sounds I've never heard before, and...and I am born again. And at dawn, we return to his hotel—he's from out of town, doing missionary work for his church back home— and he tells me I shouldn't have to go back to where I've been staying, and I know he's right, and so I go with him, and he un-makes the bed and draws the blinds so the sun won't bother me

Actor's Choice: Monologues for Women

while I sleep, and I slip under the sheets, the clean, starched, white-white sheets, and I close my eyes. And when I open them his face is there, right above mine, where it was before, he hasn't moved, he's been watching me, and I know I love him. And I reach out and he reaches out and we come together and make love. Just once. We sinned. I had been saved. And then we sinned. Well, I wanted him, and he wanted me, but we had to atone. So we made a vow. We would go back to his home, in Terre Haute, to his church, and we would marry, and I would be a good and loving wife, and he would be a good and loving husband…but we would never have intercourse again. Never. Ever. Abstinence would be our penitence. That was the price we would pay for our salvation, That is why we cannot have children.

MOTHER RUSSIA

Jeffrey Hatcher

A humorous piece about an old Russian woman remembering a celebrity obsession that she once had for a Soviet leader who visited her village once when she was young and without restraints.

KLEBB. I miss Khrushchev. I miss Brezhnev. I even miss Andropov and Chernenko. You talk about your Western televideo sex symbols, your Gyorgi Clooneys, your Yimmy Mitz, your Daveed Hasselhoff. *Soviet leaders.* These men were sexy. Watch them on the Kremlin wall on May Day…The overcoats, the gloves, the wave…

(She waves the stiff wave of a Soviet leader, then shudders in ecstasy.)

OHHHHHH! I am getting wet all over again!

(She rocks baby.)

In old days, when Soviet leader would come to village, all the women would line the streets to catch a glimpse. That's how I met Nikita. Oh, did I have a crush on that guy! "We will bury you!" he told Americans. *(Shouts:)* "*Bury me, Nikita!*" *(Calms.)* He came to our village when I was still teen-ager. I didn't sleep all night the day he came. I put my hair in the traditional tight bun, the way Nikita liked it. I wore the traditional peasant dress—grey—and worker's shoes—black—I was riot of color. I picked him red posies from the Communist Party garden, so I could throw them in his path as he came through the crowd. Did I want him? Oh, yes. Mrs. Khrushchev could pleasure him physically, but could she touch his mind? *(Beat.)* I was first woman to be at street corner where the motorcade would come by. As the hours passed and the sun rose, others joined me, other *women*, but they were Olga-Come-Latelys. They wore high heeled boots and tight workers' smocks and painted their lips with radish blossoms… *(Erupts:)* WHORES! GO BACK WHERE YOU CAME FROM, BITCHES, THIS HOT

MAN IS *MINE! (Calms.)* Then came the sound, far off at first, but coming closer, the rumble of the motorcade vibrating in my toes, my legs, going up, up—! I pressed against the barrier as the big black limo snaked and slithered through the tight narrow twists and turns! I could see the grill work now, the chrome, the hood ornament and then I saw it: the head! The round, smooth, white head, coming at me, OHMIGOD! I waved my Red Posies, my petals open and red and wet—"NIKITA! NIKITA! NIKITA!" And then…the motorcade stopped and the back window rolled down, and a stubby white hand came out of it and beckoned. I moved to the car in a trance, and as I reached toward his hand, it came out further, longer than I thought it could be…and then the First Secretary of the Communist Party, the Soviet Premier, Nikita Khrushchev, took the rich, red posies from my open palm and said: "These are from the Communist Party Garden." And they arrested me. I do not regret the time I spent in prison. The things I learned there were later useful in my work as the head of an orphanage. I know now it was Nikita's way of showing me his true feelings. Sex you can get from anybody…only a lover can put you in jail.

(Grinds out cigarette.)

O.k. So. What are we doing?

A MURDER OF CROWS

Mac Wellman

Nella, amidst the lunacy of her shouting brother and sister-in-law's clumsy attempts to comfort her, tries (unsuccessfully) to retain a shred of dignity.

NELLA. I know, I know, I know: It's my fault. If only I'd been kinder, gentler more loving and sophisticated none of this would've come to pass. I know, please forgive me for being such a fool; I know I've been a total fool with my life, all of it, including getting poor and homeless after his death and having to impose like this, on the good will of relations, my dear brother and my sister-in-law, both of you, successful and clear-sighted and pillars of the community, and far above Susannah and me, poor folks who ought to be swept under the rug, or otherwise disposed of, as one would do with garbage, cat-litter or moldy old clothes, clothes not even fit for the Salvation army.

(Pause.)

Fate stinks, on the whole, I would say. Although I am proud. I am not bitter. Bitterness is for drunkards, prostitutes, and the unemployed who do not even try to go out and find a job of real work to do, as for instance, in the service industry or something, even at the grease pit where they hire Arabs and other Asiatic filths because no white person will lower himself to stoop to that horrid, putrid slime and actually lift whole shovels-ful of the awful stuff and drop it, ick! in the wheelbarrow and not faint from the reek with some man in a fez standing nearby, grinning wide, his teeth blackened—the ones that haven't been kicked out in fights over gypsy women, liquor and the dice in some ramshackle Asiatic bazaar. And him not doing a lick of work, while your heart goes boing! boing! as if you had fallen from a high place and hit the pavement. I'm sorry about all of it, and I know I'm to blame.

A MURDER OF CROWS

Mac Wellman

Georgia, possessing a clean prophecy of America, attempts to justify her hatred of her husband's sister.

GEORGIA. Alright, alright. I know you're right, and when you talk like that, all you do is further humiliate me, and that's alright too, I'm used to it, I don't mind, I can take it, and it won't be the first time. Only Howard, I have a vision of how good America could be, if only it weren't for your family, particularly that part of it currently residing in our house, because America deserves better than this, I mean this overcrowded, down-in-the-dumps, small-time depression atmosphere, it just doesn't hit the nail on the head, it's not up to snuff, furthermore it's bothersome and a crying shame. And I know we've got to be hospitable even when we don't give a crap, but why oh why must they smell so bad, Jesus, Howard, it drives me crazy, the way they stink. That's not normal. All the people in Michigan can't smell like that. There must be something wrong with their insides to make a stench like that. They're eating our food, so it can't be that, our food is good, normal American-type food. Nothing too unusual, nothing too spicy. They bathe, don't they? I mean, I've seen evidence of them bathing, so it can't be that. Maybe they only pretend to bathe, is that possible? Howard, could they be THAT INSANE that they would only pretend to bathe, but secretly not bathe?

A MURDER OF CROWS

Mac Wellman

Susannah, alone and intense, prays to whoever and whatever dark forces (and light ones) to change the world she so much despises.

SUSANNAH. I wish Aunt Georgia and Uncle Howard would drop dead, sweet Jesus, or please, PLEASE! at least be disfigured horribly by acid, or heavy machinery. I wish they would die very soon, and go away, and leave us the shopping bags of money which they have hidden I know not where. I wish a general pox on all their houses. Except for that part of the house we live in, Mom and me, and the dog;—fuck the dog!—fuck the dog, and let him sizzle in the fires of hell also—; but save our dear kitty: Lucifer Ornamental Pokum, dearer to me than anyone, or anything. Because, sweet Jesus, who dwells in the fullness of the clouds and the mist, in the rain, in the sleet, in the snow, and even in the rich amber filigree of the twilight, these relations, all of them, both, are wicked, tactless, vicious, nosey, cheap, sleazy, cornball, sadistic even, and not with it, not with it in a way that I find totally…boring.

(Pause.)

They do not correspond to the picture of humanity I have formed in my head. All they think about is local politics, the eighth race at Aqueduct, and taxes. Taxes and the price of oil. They think about money too much, and are always complaining about how they need more of it. They make mother and me feel like freeloaders and bums and homeless people, just because we have no money and no place to live. If my father were still alive he would sweep down upon them with his anger and fire and iron thorns and flails, and destroy them like the Indians. He would roar out of the TV set and leap upon them and slit their throats, and mutilate their bodies and roast them until they were burnt to a crisp. Then he would stomp on their ashes till there was nothing remaining but a hideous black smudge on the carpet of the livingroom. Livingroom! A place I loathe and look down upon. A "livingroom" possesses no climate in general, and no weather to speak of. A livingroom is like Andy: a useless relic of a long-gone historical moment. I am not among my kind, and do not even know what my kind are. I feel strange.

MY LEFT BREAST

Susan Miller

Susan, who has had a mastectomy, has—for the first time—referred to herself as a gay woman while meeting with her therapist. She ruminates about this.

SUSAN. Because, I want to say, when you're a hurt and leaky thing, all definitions are off. What you were, who you told everyone you might be had a sheen, the spit of artifice. There was always something covert. But now, you've come apart. Like an accident victim in shock, you don't see who sees you and you don't care how you are seen. You are a creature, simply. You move or stop or lurch from side to side as you are able. You make a sound without will. Your former self, the husk of you, hovering near, looks on startled and concerned. But you are not. You are shorn of image. You are waiting to eat again and to speak in a language with meaning. You are not gay. You are not a woman. You are not. And by this, you are everything your former self defended against, apologized for, explained away, took pride in. You are all of it. None of it. You want only to breathe in and out. And know what your limbs will do. You are at the beginning.

NEVER TELL

James Christy

Liz is a 14 year old recounting a traumatic visit from her uncle Sam. The speech is part of a flashback and should be performed by an adult (in the play Liz is in her late 20s).

LIZ. It was last summer. My dad had a birthday party for my mom and her brother Sam came. Uncle Sam. When he'd see us, he'd point his finger at us and yell out "I want you" and give us these painful bear hugs. So he was drinking bourbon and telling us this story about this guy who used to work with him at his shop. Every Friday they'd go to this local bar and have beers with their lunch. So one day the guy got really drunk, and when they got back my uncle told him he should be careful 'cause they work with all this heavy machinery. And the guy laughs and says he's fine. And like five minutes later the guy slices off three of his fingers. He was so drunk he said it didn't even hurt, he just felt warm blood on his hands. On the way to the hospital he was holding up his middle finger and pointing it at my uncle and laughing. It was kinda sad 'cause he got fired and didn't even get worker's comp because he was drunk and all. But the way Uncle Sam told it it was so funny.

(Beat.)

I went up to bed but I could still hear him and my mom as I watched a movie in my room. John Cusack was talking to some girl, I fell half-asleep and started dreaming that he was talking to me. And in the dream he was looking at me and saying something and it was perfect, you know? Right then I looked up and my uncle Sam was in my room. He just stood there watching the John Cusack movie for a long time. Then he asked me if I had a boyfriend and I said no. And he said that was a shame because he thought I was pretty. I knew he was drunk and I knew it wasn't right that he was in my room but it seemed like he meant it. And then he came into my bed. And I said that he should go but he told me I knew he wasn't going to go and I should just be quiet. And when he was doing it I remember being surprised that I could still hear the movie. I thought it was supposed to be louder with grunting and stuff but I could still hear John Cusack like before. And when he was done he got up and put his hand on my hair and said it would be our secret. But he said it like he knew it already, he knew I wouldn't tell. And he was right, I haven't. And I won't.

NEVER TELL

James Christy

Anne is a 14 year old describing an awkward sexual experience on her 13th birthday. The speech is part of a flashback and should be performed by an adult (in the play Anne is in her late 20s).

ANNE. I don't like getting older. Everyone's so eager about it, I really don't see why. It doesn't seem that great to me.

(Sighs.)

It was during my birthday party last June. I had told Donald he could touch them when I was fourteen because that's when my best friend let her boyfriend touch hers. And he thought it should be, like, that night, on my birthday. So even though all my aunts and uncles were there we went up to my room and I locked the door. And he was so serious about it. We didn't make out or anything. He was just looking at them, and then he watched his hands go on them sort of in slow motion. And maybe he was nervous, but it seemed like he did it like I wasn't there. I always thought with guys that you'd know when it was right. If you liked them and they liked you whatever stuff like that you'd do, as long as you waited and everything, it'd be okay. But I was standing there with Donald—who I liked, who was cute and funny and nice to my little brother—and he was touching me like I was a science experiment. And I got this feeling that the next day he'd be laughing about it and bragging to his friends. And I started thinking, you know, is it always like this? Where you don't know what they're thinking, you just have to guess all the time.

NICE TIE

Rich Orloff

*A woman at a bar has just been asked by a man if he can buy her a drink.
She's the type to always think several moves ahead.*

WOMAN. Oh, I don't know. First you buy me a drink, and then
we get to chatting, and if we're not too bored with each other, you
ask for my phone number, and I figure what the hell, so I give it to
you. If you don't call me, I'm disappointed. If you do call me, we
go out, and either I don't like you, or I like you and you don't like
me. And I'm disappointed. Or we do like each other, and we go out
some more, and things become pretty wonderful—great sex, revealing conversations, compatible neuroses—but I discover I want
more than you can give. And I'm disappointed.

Or we stay with it, and we get closer and closer and more in love
and more dependent on each other, which gives us the strength to
go through periods of emotional turmoil, mutual doubts, and
things said in anger that we'll pretend to forget but which will come
up again during the post-natal depression I'll have after the birth of
our first child. *If* we get married, that is, and Lord knows how many
friends I'll lose because they like me but they're just not comfortable around you.

After our second child, the unresolved conflicts we buried for the
sake of our marriage will propel you into a torrid affair, either with
someone you work with or, God forbid, one of my few friends
who *is* comfortable around you. I'll try to forgive you, eventually,
and either you'll resent the obligation of a monogamous relationship, or you'll try to become philosophical about it, by which point
both our children will be in intensive therapy. The divorce will be
ugly, expensive, and years later than it should've been. I'll never be
able to trust men again, those who aren't frightened off by my

sagging features and two sadomasochistic children. The kids'll blame me, of course, and I'll die all alone… I think I'll pass on the drink. It's a nice offer, but the pain just isn't worth it.

Nice tie, though.

O'KEEFFE!

Lucinda McDermott

Georgia worries that much of her success is the result of her husband Alfred Stieglist, the photographer. She fumes about the sacrifices she has made for her art and for Alfred.

GEORGIA O'KEEFFE. Alfred!

One of your sister's children just called me Aunt Georgia!

…Well, I slapped the stupid thing and said don't ever, ever call me Aunt Georgia again!

…I don't care! We lived together almost eight years before we were married, I wasn't Aunt Georgia then! What difference does a piece of paper make?

…I have no right? You won't let me have a child of my own—a family of my own—you have denied me the pulse of life itself—I will not allow your nieces and nephews to call me Aunt!

…You can be Uncle Alfred and love it and go to hell for all I care—you and your huge ugly family! I have had to cut off certain parts of myself—to be the woman you want me to be.

…Yes—you are probably right. I am sure you are. The art would suffer if I was a mother. But Alfred, certain things go deeper than just a want—desires are not always creations of our own.

Remember when we went to see *Macbeth*? Remember I cried when she said:

I have given suck, and know
How tender 'tis to love the babe that milks me.
I would, while it was smiling in my face,
Have plucked my nipple from his boneless gums
And dashed the brains out, had I so sworn as you

Have done to this.

I know that feeling. I have killed my babies because I have killed my desire for them. I did it for the art. I did it for you. But you must understand—a certain sensitivity died as well. For children, for family and family things. Silly things. Sweet things.

…I have to get out of here. Leave Lake George.

…I can't spend another summer here. Children running in and out—playing in my paints—that one destroyed canvas!

Noise, noise, noise! People, people, people! There's no peace!

…Well, you must make yourself understand. This cannot be a battle of wills Alfred, my survival is at stake here.

…I can't paint!

…I don't know where I'll go. New Mexico. I don't know. I only know that I must go.

…What will you do without me? One can only guess.

OVER THE TAVERN

Tom Dudzick

The year is 1959. In an unusual Parent-Teacher Conference, an old Catholic nun confesses a dark secret to the father of one of her students.

SISTER. Chester, there was no childhood accident with a boxcar door. It was your father. <u>He</u> broke your fingers. Silence, listen to me. After the railroad guard dragged you home that day, your father came to see me. He was quite upset. He wanted to know what he should do with this boy of his who steals from trains. I was young, but I had just broken the Lucenti boy's habit of driving other people's cars, so I spoke with your father. I pointed out the dangers of leniency. I even demonstrated my technique with a ruler. He thanked me, went on his way and that was that. A sincere man; I liked him. I wasn't aware at the time that he drank. The next morning I saw your bandages. The novitiate hadn't prepared me for this. After dismissal I ran to Reverend Mother and told her what I'd caused. I didn't think God could ever forgive me. "Tell me what to do, Mother!" "Satan is relentless in his pursuit of these children," she said, "so our resolve must be just as strong. Do nothing, Sister. This is how we save their souls." I ran to that chapel and prayed all night. I begged God for some kind of answer. Silence. As if God were telling me to be silent; just do as I'm told. So I lived with the image that had been burned into my mind— your little bandaged hand. What did your father use? It wasn't a ruler. Ah. A broom handle. I am sorry. I prayed for your recovery. For years I prayed. But last night in your home I realized that all the prayer in the world couldn't undo my original sin of silence. Reverend Mother was wrong. I should have said something, done something forty years ago. It's still going on. No, no, of course. You don't hit your children. But rulers and broomsticks aren't the only things that damage.

PASSIVE BELLIGERENCE

Stephen Belber

Two men with opposite demeanors have just been interviewed for the same job: Gail's full-time lover. Gail runs down a list of qualifications that they must possess in order to meet her needs—needs which her husband hasn't been able to fulfill.

GAIL. Good, good. *(Putting résumé down, addressing them both:)* Well as I said, I'm a little pressed for time today. I told myself that I would hire someone by—*(Looking at watch)* —five o'clock, and here it is, five o'clock, I think I've interviewed sixty people already and I still can't seem to find someone I like. But you're both pleasant surprises and both very qualified so I feel like I'm almost there. So, thanks for that.

As you can probably imagine, when I asked myself what the qualities were that I was looking for in a full-time lover, a number of variables presented themselves to me. To begin with, availability. My husband and I have only been married a year but he's already begun avoiding his corporeal responsibility to me. Maybe he's got someone else, power to him if he does, all I know is that he's putting in 65-hour weeks down there at Paine Webber which really doesn't leave him with the time and energy required to properly service his wife. And the fact is, this little car needs more than the occasional tune-up.

Secondly, I need imagination. For all of the indubitably imaginative financial flourishes that Jim whips out as he climbs the corporate ladder, the man has nary whipped out a ball of twine thus far with his wife, to say nothing of ankle chains or the occasional prison warden routine. And so I seek creativity. And let us not forget adventurism, foresight and, of course, foreplay, although I'm not one of these women who get carried away with the conceit. My philosophy since the eighth grade has been: put the sausage in the oven while the coal's still hot, and stoke, for God's sake, stoke, stoke!

And yet, thirdly, I need someone who challenges me, not just sexually—although mostly sexually—but also emotionally and intellectually. Jim's good with numbers but the man couldn't write a poem to save his life, much less recite *The Wasteland* while mounting me from behind. You can both take note of that.

So I think that essentially what I'm looking for is a well-endowed man—and please don't interpret that in a merely juvenile way, for I mean well-endowed in every sense of the phrase, most notably in terms of integrity. *(To* Dan:*)* I like a man who can sit here and tell me that he's into passivity; *(To* Jeff:*)* or a man who's not afraid to admit that he has a violent streak, especially when he has no idea that it's a perfect qualification for the job he's just applied for. So that's nice, but I still have one very important question I'd like to put forth to you gentlemen: Why do you think you should have this job?

PERMANENT COLLECTION

Thomas Gibbons

Kanika Weaver, a young African-American woman, has been thrust into the struggle for control of an art museum between her boss, the museum's African-American director, and Paul Barrow, the white education director. She attempts to clarify her confused feelings.

KANIKA. A few days ago I was in the mall at Eighth and Spring. They were having a Black Art Expo—you know the kind I mean. Paintings of heroic black men with bulging muscles…serene mothers lifting their children up to the sun. Everyone looking proud and regal and *strong*.

All right, you can laugh. You know what? I did too. Part of me. I know now it's not good art—thanks to you. Not like Cezanne and Matisse. I shouldn't say that, I guess. I mean, I'm not *supposed* to feel that way, am I? *(Pause.)* But when I looked at those paintings… I could see myself. My body, my hair, my skin. They *acknowledged* me. And the paintings at the Foundation—you have to admit, Paul—they don't.

> *(Suddenly she is close to tears, but she rushes on, intent on making him understand:)*

I'm not saying those painters you love were racists, you know I'm not. No one is saying that. They were painting their world, the one they saw, I understand that. But how do you think it makes me feel, to be surrounded by all that *whiteness?*

You never asked, did you?

You never wanted to know.

PLAYING HOUSE

Brooke Berman

Wendy, a pragmatic healer, talks matter-of-factly about how she had to first overcome severe bouts of depression before receiving her "gift" of healing, which she uses to help others.

WENDY. This is how I became a healer. I went to Hell and I came back with a gift. I came back able to see into people and objects and the Earth and to move things inside of them. But, first I was in Hell. Like you. And, it was bad. I didn't get out of bed for a long time. I pretended I was a bear and that it was winter, and I hibernated. I went on food stamps and unemployment, and I sold things. Just to support my sleep habit. But I trusted and did what my insides told me to. I took naps all the time, every day. And I cried a lot. In bed, in the bathtub, in Central Park, in the A&P buying groceries. Actually, I never shopped at the A&P, but you know what I mean, right? Anyway, miraculous things began to occur. While I was asleep, the light got in and moved things inside of me. It was amazing. The healing occurred while I was not conscious. I woke up and had this gift. And I'd always had it only I couldn't find it before. But once I found it, I could use it to help people. To set them on their path. I believe in change. I believe in healing. I believe you can make great progress in this life.

Poof!

Lynn Nottage

Loureen struggles with feelings of guilt and jubilation over her abusive husband's recent death and her newfound freedom.

LOUREEN. Everybody always told me, "Keep your place, Loureen." My place, the silent spot on the couch with a wine cooler in my hand and a pleasant smile that warmed the heart. All this time I didn't know why he was so afraid for me to say anything, to speak up. Poof! …I've never been by myself, except for them two weeks when he won the office pool and went to Reno with his cousin Mitchell. He wouldn't tell me where he was going until I got that postcard with the cowboy smoking a hundred cigarettes… Didn't Sonny Larkin look good last week at Caroline's? He looked good, didn't he…

(*FLORENCE nods. She nervously picks up Samuel's jacket, which is hanging on the back of the chair. She clutches it unconsciously.*)

NO! No! Don't wrinkle that, that's his favorite jacket. He'll kill me. Put it back!

(*FLORENCE returns the jacket to its perch. LOUREEN begins to quiver.*)

I'm sorry. (*She grabs the jacket and wrinkles it up:*) There! (*She then digs into the coat pockets and pulls out his wallet and a movie stub.*) Look at that, he said he didn't go to the movies last night. Working late. (*Frantically thumbs through his wallet:*) Picture of his motorcycle, Social Security card, driver's license, and look at that from our wedding. (*Smiling.*) I looked good, didn't I? (*She puts the pictures back in the wallet and holds the jacket up to her face.*) There were some good things. (*She then sweeps her hand over the jacket to remove the wrinkles, and folds it ever so carefully, and finally throws it in the garbage:*) And out of my mouth those words made him disappear. All these years and just words, Florence. That's all they were.

THE POTATO CREEK CHAIR OF DEATH

Robert Kerr

Valerie is an elderly woman who has been traveling throughout the United States with her son, Cedric, ever since he won a multi-million dollar sweepstakes. In the course of their travels, they have repeatedly encountered Michael, a teenage runaway. Cedric, sensing a connection forming between Michael and Valerie, has jealously and manipulatively kept Michael and Valerie apart. In this scene, Michael has just discovered Valerie wandering along a back road late at night in bloodstained clothes. Valerie tells Michael how she has extricated herself from her relationship with her possessive son.

VALERIE. They'll find the car in the morning. I have to be far away. You have to help me. You have to understand. He always… He had this way of… Whenever he was around there was hardly room for me to even breathe.

He wanted to use the phone, but I wouldn't let him. I hit him hard on the nose. He has hemophilia. I knew that, but in that split second I forgot. I hit him all over. I just didn't stop. He had bruises everywhere. He was so surprised and so delicate he didn't stop me. He just collapsed and started to cry. I stopped and said I'd take him to the hospital. I didn't know where the hospital was, of course, but I was so scared and so sad and so confused I thought we could just keep driving until we found it. He was sitting next to me with blood coming out of his nose and his skin turning funny colors. After a while I noticed he had stopped crying. He was just sitting up in the seat. Not moving. So I just kept driving until the car ran out of gas.

I did love him, I think. I don't know. As bad as…as awful as this sounds… When I was hitting Cedric, and hitting him and hitting him… Something came from somewhere, while I was hitting him.

A feeling, not since I was… Something I thought was lost forever. Something alive. I can't let it waste away. I can't get caught.

I need you to give me a ride. Wherever you are going.

PROCLIVITIES

Kirsten Greenidge

Georgia, a pregnant waitress, never enjoyed going to the library when she was young because of the way the school librarians had treated her. Now that she's an adult, Georgia makes daily trips to the library to insure that her unborn child gets to take advantage of the books in ways she never could.

GEORGIA. Every day?: I go to the library. Which doesn't sound like much. I know. But it is. Because. I used to hate the library. Because. Of that hour. That library hour. In school. And I absolutely hated it. I would have rather have had my eyes scratched out. I wasn't one of those cute kids: patent leather; ankle socks; ribbons. I was: I was one of those kids: who always has something around their mouth. Like dirt. Or juice. Juice would do it every time. Leave a ring that stayed all day. So those ladies, those library ladies, they didn't enjoy me. They said my hands were sticky, they said I'd ruin the pictures on the pages of the books. And that's all a kid wants, right, that's all a kid: to just run your fingers over those shiny pages. *Mike Mulligan and His Steam Shovel*, and Eloise, whose shirt was always untucked, and that retarded monkey who hung out with the skinny guy in yellow and was always messing everything up: all I wanted was to be able to reach out and touch those people, well, that monkey wasn't a person, and that steam shovel was metal, but all I wanted was to be able to feel the shine of those pages on my fingers, have that library book smell stay on their tips until after lunch when they'd smell like left over milk again, which, I guess, matched the smell around my mouth. But those mothy ladies. I could see them watching me over the pages, when they'd take the half a second to turn the pages and they'd look, I know, I could see, I could feel, they'd look down at me and stare at that ring around my mouth, the dirt under my nails. Once, one even reached out, reached out to me in the front, I loved the front, not only the clean kids should be able to sit in the front, and she reached out with her thumb, after she'd licked it to turn the page, she rubbed the corner of my mouth, and those other kids, they didn't even blink, I wished one of them maybe would have laughed, cause then, well, then it wouldn't've been like it was *expected*, like it was *normal*, for some old bat to be wiping my face off in front of the whole entire class. And her thumb, the spit on her thumb smelled like hell, like her jaws opened up into—but what do I care now, right?, I mean I guess the whole library room had that smell, like the air in my grandma's shoes. Not the slippers. The loafers. Down by the toe part. Where the sweat goes. Who wants to read if you're going to stink like a loafer after? Not me. Stupid mothy library ladies. But, I don't give a crap now, you know? Now I actually like going to the library. Every day. I pick a different book. And I open it to the middle, and I place it on my stomach. I balance it. I let whoever's in here absorb it. And I stay like that. For hours.

QUAKE

Melanie Marnich

The present time. While Lucy and her boyfriend sleep, Lucy dreams her first dream of That Woman ("an astrophysicist gone bad"). This is the dream that launches That Woman into Lucy's psyche and reality. Here, That Woman explains the passion, power and confusion that make her unique—and that fuel her and Lucy's journeys for the rest of the play.

WOMAN. Like most scientific pioneers, I do my boldest work in near isolation. Like most scientific pioneers, I'm called a crackpot. Like most scientific pioneers, I'm out of a job. Unlike most scientific pioneers, I have to dispose of a body. I am fucking brilliant. And that is pure energy. Energy doesn't disappear. Cannot disappear. Never ever. It's transferred. It's an undeniable force. It's nature. It's science. It's out of my hands. I loved each one. Then there's that minute you look at him and wonder who? Why? Why don't you love me like you used to? Where did it go? It can't disappear. It's energy. It must be somewhere. These guys… They were only human, and I knew what it was like to wish upon a supernova.

I just wanted more.

THE REBIRTH OF BEAUTIFUL

John Walch

Puppet Mary vents her alter-ego's inner frustration and ambivalence about her depressive husband, Joseph, who has been pressuring Mary to have a baby.

PUPPET MARY. He's always dropping hints. The pressure is killing me. He says he wants a baby, but what he wants is a distraction. A distraction from his life. I work, I have a life. I want a life and a child. He wants a child to become his life. He got "laid-off" a year ago. Fired is what really happened. The ax. Canned. And now he refuses to get a job. He says: "there are no jobs." He's a cook, for god's-sake. People don't eat anymore? The meals he used to cook. God, the smells that used to fill this house. But now he won't even cook. He just makes frozen-dinners. That's it. A gourmet chef, heating up frozen-dinners. But he has all the time in the world to clean out closets, dream up names for a dreamed of baby, wipe adjectives from his brain, and turn a leaf into a shelf. Oh, he has time for puppets too. Another of his therapist's recommendations. This was the doctor's advice: "Make puppets. Puppets that are honest. Puppets that speak the truth." Here's your truth, Joseph: you want a baby *from* me, not *with* me. And sometimes I think…

…I want a divorce, not a baby.

RED DEATH

Lisa D'Amour

Connie Albright is on a yacht with her husband Prospero. A few minutes ago, she passed out when their maid revealed herself to be the woman who killed their daughter, Lucy. Connie's life passes before her eyes.

CONNIE. I see the green grass round Grass Lake. And then I am in my hometown and there is the bicycle my father bought me when I was five years old, and the knee I skinned learning to ride it. And hello there I am junior prom queen! This is the way one sips a drink, this is the way one waves goodbye. Boo hoo my reign is over! Anyway it's almost just as good, sitting alone in my room making paper cut-outs of the girl I wish I was. The hips are adequate but it's what is inside that counts: that extraordinary flame in the center of my ribs. The bus towards California is moldy and crowded, but I must get away: I am making my way in the world. Anyway one day I will have my own girl. I am making rice I am making yellow squash I am selling my first house I am making peas. And when he is down on one knee before me there is a flash and I am back inside the oval of my baby bassinet. I am a baby and everything is light, my eyes are wide and through the primary colors of the mobile I see a woman crying hard and she reaches towards me with the handful of powder and pat pat pats my belly and it feels exquisite but her tears won't stop they drop drop drop on my soft skin. And then I realize, this is it—

> *(Quick, PROSPERO hits CONNIE, hard, on the back of her head with a chair or some other heavy object. It is super fast and super violent. CONNIE is out cold. PROSPERO picks her up, walks to the side of the yacht, and lowers her into the water.)*

ROCK SCISSORS PAPER

Deb Margolin

A Girl remembers a family trip to Mount Rushmore after her brother's death. She speaks even the most revealing lines without a hint of self-consciousness.

GIRL. Whatever my mother's looking for is always *behind* her. I've noticed that. It never fucking fails. Whatever she can't find is always where her ass is. I'm upstairs, and she's screaming where the hell is *whatever it is,* and I'm just like, Mom, turn around! Just turn around, Mom! They say mothers have eyes in the back of their heads—well, yeah, right! My mom has trouble with the two in front! Once she was like, I smell fire, and she's looking around sniffing, and the garbage can was on fire right where her butt was but she just never turned around.

We took this family vacation recently to Rapid City, South Dakota, which even the name Rapid City is pretty funny, and we tried to act like a family, only we all just based it on shows on TV. Trouble was, we all used different shows. For my mom it was like, Bill Cosby show, where the wife is some dignified Doctor, for my dad it was *Home Improvement,* and for me it was like, *Roseanne.* So it was like three shows playing at once. Pretty bad. I wish my brother were still alive. We fought like dogs but when he died it was like when a kid gets off the seesaw real fast without telling you and you're the one who's up in the air on the other side. I hate that he died, I just hate it. He once gave me this dirty picture, he said he got it from Joey diFlorio, this tough kid at school. It was really small, this picture, it was like, black and white and all, and my brother said it was a real picture of people doing it that Joey took himself, even though it was printed on like newspaper or something. Anyhow, I still have that picture, and it's like my brother whispering in my ear, laughing.

SELF DEFENSE,
OR DEATH OF SOME SALESMEN

Carson Kreitzer

Jolene Palmer (JO) is a prostitute on death row for the killing of seven johns.

JO. I told her she should quit her job, 'cos she was making like 150 bucks a week and I was making like 150 bucks a *day*. When I went out. And it was no problem you know, I… I wanted to take care a her.

I liked it that I was able to…that there was somebody I could take care of.

An' you could get all…psychological about it if you want, say it's on account of that baby I had when I was fourteen, that they took away.

(Laughs.)

You'd think I'd learn my lesson. That was the first time I got raped in a car. Cuttin' school, trippin' on acid and a quaalude. Didn't want to go to the cops 'cos I thought they'd know. Give me a blood test or some shit, throw me in jail. Saw that motherfucker around town all the time. He saw me, gettin' big. Musta known. I didn't tell nobody who it was. You'd think you could get in a car with a friend of your dad, right? Somebody you've seen around the house? But you can't…you can't let 'em kill you. You know? You gotta beat it.

Anyway, you could say it was because of that, but I don't think that's it. I think it's simpler than that.

An' she's just the most…good…person I've ever met in my whole life. She's one person out of this whole goddamned life that's actually a good person. And I was just glad I could take care of her.

SELF DEFENSE,
OR DEATH OF SOME SALESMEN

Carson Kreitzer

The Coroner has seen a lot. She is a highly rational person, which usually gets her through.

CORONER. I've seen a lot of dead prostitutes, in my line of work. A lot. And it's not supposed to be something you get upset about. I am a doctor, after all. A doctor of the dead. And it's like cancer or something, as a doctor, you're not supposed to get upset about it. Curse God or— You're supposed to speak in calm, rational terms. Not alarm the patient. Comfort the family.

A coroner's main job is to listen.

Find out how this thing happened. Make the call.

Natural causes. Suicide. Homicide.

And these girls who come in, ripped up some of 'em in ways that speak of a hatred I can barely begin to comprehend.

I've been listening to their bodies. For years. Listening to stories of desecrations of the human body not to mention the spirit that I can only call evil. Although I never had much of a dialogue with God or any sort of metaphysical thing. Suddenly I am forced to have this conception of evil. This knowledge.

The listening—adds up. Sometimes I feel it is eroding me, like a high whistling wind over sandstone. I am becoming…mute and rough and rounded.

I didn't come to this job with any fancy ideas about justice. The…orderliness appealed to me. The ability to find truths. Add detail upon detail, layering to conclusion.

Without too many people cluttering things up, if you want to know the truth. I…have a little trouble dealing with people. Figured I could do my job, do it well, have a large degree of privacy in my life. These things are important to me.

The ideas about justice—started springing up at me. After the bodies had been piling up. For a while. Girls, women, who should not have been on my table. Sure, I get some ODs, suicides, but it's the others. The ones who shouldn't have been on my table for another forty years. Who should never have gone through what they went through to get to my table. And they're whispering to me—

Unsolved. unsolved. unsolved. unsolved.

SPLIT

Allison Moore

Lisa, a bubbly, slightly naive single mother in her late 20s, asks her co-worker to cover a shift at the factory.

LISA. I think my daughter is going to go to the Olympics. That's why I need the shift covered. I mean, it's a ways off. She's only eight. But in other countries, in China or Russia, they have scouts, who visit schools and identify, exceptional children? And when they find them, they're like moved so they can train with the masters. Mr. Sawicki, Kelly's gym teacher, he told me about it. He said we don't really do that in America, but he said Kelly could definitely get a track scholarship for private high school. And private school would be good, because, you know, Park High is pretty rough. I don't really understand why we don't do it here, you know, work with younger kids? I mean, if they're doing it in China. America is definitely better than China, right? But Mr. Sawicki said there are programs, special summer camps. But I looked on the Internet and they're, expensive. I'm up to $11.50 an hour now, which is pretty good. We always have everything we need, I'm proud of that. When I was pregnant with Kelly, my dad said I should have an abortion. He said it would be better not to bring her into the world, because, because there was no way he was going to help me and I would never be able to support her and give her what she needs, and then it would be two lives wasted instead of just one, he said. He was talking about me, of course, but. Kelly's the best thing I've ever done. And ever will do. I'm not, exceptional. But Kelly is. I just know it. So I'm going to do whatever I have to, to make sure that the world sees how special she is. Maybe that's the one thing I could do. I could be an exceptional mom to this really extra-exceptional kid.

SPRING

Tanya Palmer

While helping fit her daughter into a prom dress, Wendy's mother reminisces about her own prom night, including the strange fear caused by the looming sky.

WENDY'S MOTHER. In my time, the colour was mauve. All the girls were wearing it. Mauve bows, mauve gloves, mauve corsages, mauve handbags. I had a passion for colors, so I would try to experiment. Dark mauve, light mauve, whatever I could get away with. On my seventeenth birthday I wore a light mauve skirt with a dark mauve sweater set, pinkish shoes and a purplish bow in my hair; I did like to be different. That must be where you got that rebellious streak from. For prom I wore a hoop skirt and a train too, in a nice rich mauve that matched my garter belt. Turn this way dear. There'd been a storm the night before, and all day the light was strange. I spent a full half hour just staring out the window watching the clouds move, change shape and colour. Then my date came to pick me up, Rick Nusmeir is his name, he's a district attorney now. As we were getting out of the car in the high school parking lot, everything got very dark, and the whole sky, everything, turned this beautiful deep purple, not mauve at all, almost black, and the clouds came down so far, I felt as if I was kissing them. It was terrifying, I don't know why, what's a little cloud going to do to you? But I grasped onto Rick's arm and started to cry. My mascara ran a bit but I had a tissue tucked behind my watch so I fixed it up without too much trouble. Rick was real understanding although I'm sure he thought I was a bit soft. The strangest thing was, with my mauve dress and pumps and accessories, it was like I was a lighter version of the sky. And for a moment, there by the car, it felt like it could just swallow me up, and I'd become vapour, just like those clouds, that's all they are really, just some other form of water, and that to me was the most terrifying thing I've ever experienced.

THE SUBWAY

John Augustine

Following various ordinary panhandlers in a New York subway, this effervescent, upbeat (and unrealistic), Real Estate Woman takes a chance and pitches to the trapped subway riders all the good properties she has in New York City.

REAL ESTATE WOMAN. May I have your attention please? I do not rob. I do not steal. I'm in REAL ESTATE. And I have a lovely apartment listed on the upper west side. It has an eat in kitchen and lovely pre-war features, although it is a modern building. It has several closets that COULD be knocked down to create the FEELING of space. It doesn't have a doorman, but there is room for one. You don't see many door women. Why is that I wonder? Ladies! Perk up your ears. I just created more job opportunities for us. Now then. The main room can be used as a living room or a bedroom. It's very versatile. I think it would be a lovely meditation room because it is so WONderfully dark. There is one small window, but you could easily board that up with a book case. Or…for those of you who are not day sleepers, you could easily install several very large picture windows with board approval. God knows what you'd look at. Crack dealers welcome! In fact, I have some good crack for sale right now. Just kidding. That's my sense of humor. Isn't it good? So if everybody would gather by the far door, we can all get off at the next stop and I'll be conducting a walking tour of the upper west side. Bring your check books!

SWOOP

Mac Wellman

First Mina, soaring far above the earth and occasionally swooping down to feed, observes the meaningless rules that govern the world.

FIRST MINA. Sometimes I feel as though I had been swimming in time, as though it were a clear fluid. A palpable substance, both hindering and supporting one's motor control. Decades like waves in the ocean, beating upon a shore that is the Inconceivable. The rush of meaningless events, wars, atrocities, the useless obsession with dates, facts, and slightly prurient information concerning one's neighbors. The hideous redundancy of fashion, with its vapid and supercilious alternation of hats, ideas, shoes, and highflown rhetoric. Its shabby conceits. The sanctimonious pursuit of what is called "truth" by the parsimonious inheritors of wealth, power, privilege or other idiotic additive tropisms. Lust for the finite. The endless mediocre puppet show of apparent choice versus apparent error. The cruel slaughter of innocence in the name of stupidity, and even innocence… A thing of no worth…like a flashlight buried in muck, at the bottom of the sea.

(Pause.)

For in truth we do inhabit a world of blur, a world of vague, insubstantial entities, and this is apparent once one has had the nerve to harden oneself a bit, and examine what passes for reality with a little critical…with a little skepticism. All the hubbub of the Moving World amounts to mere perturbation, a slightly exasperating surface tension vertically rendered on the horizontal face of a small, insignificant pond that is quietly freezing over.

Wilhelmina. Mina. Strange, I do not seem able to recall my own last name. My patronymic. The name of my father. Who was my father, for in truth I possess none, now that I am *vlkoslak,* undead, one of the High Ladies of Ckm Ckm. A world adrift inhabited by evil cats and evil cockatoos the color of pure ionization. Butterflies with razor wings. Gigantic palaces of time-mottled chert and schist, draculan towers of adamant, floating above the streaming rubble of the red wind. Magyar music rattling up from cisterns of Empty Time out of antique celestas and barrel organs. *Vlkoslak,* vampire. A world like a child's spinning top, spinning so rapidly as to appear quite motionless. A world beyond the palaver of easy comprehension.

Swoop

Mac Wellman

Second Mina, teeth aching, muses about her eating habits and her post-bite life.

SECOND MINA. I have returned, and am different. I am the same, but different.

(Pause.)

Although the truth is, I was not the one who bit: I was bitten. Not that I have any problem with who I am. Nope, not me. And my teeth hurt. Biting is hard on teeth, and I'm no spring chicken, I know. Maybe I'll have to stop eating housecats. Maybe eating housecats has ruined my teeth. Would you get a load of my teeth. Big Choppers. I used to have these dainty, white, pearly teeth. The kind moonstruck poets used to write about. But after my "turn," that's a miserable euphemism for being bitten—after my turn my teeth got big and nasty. Maybe I'll have to give up eating plump, white housecats. Really is a disgusting habit, if you think about it. Maybe I'll just give up eating tomcats. Tomcats really are rancid. They disgust even me. I'm not without compunctions. Only, it's hard to tell them apart from seven miles up on a cold and partly-cloudy moonlit night. You can just barely make them out because the earth gives off a faint, preternatural glow. As though it were alive. Giordano Bruno thought the world was alive. They burnt him at the stake in February 1600 in Rome. I was there, in the *Campo di Fiori,* in 1600. The "Field of Flowers" in English. It was a fairly cold day. A day like one of Giotto's frescoes. The reality of it bursting from newly wrought lines of mathematical perspective. I thought I saw the Pope, Clement VIII, but it probably wasn't him. Anyhow, I watched Bruno sizzle. I was glad they roasted him. The heretic. He knew too much. People who know too much all ought to burn. He said the earth moves because it is alive. That's enough for me. Burn the heretic. Freedom of speech for those who can afford it, and those who watch what they say. I know what I'm talking about, since being who I am, with these big monster teeth, I nose about in places most people don't even know exist, and therefore have no conception of. Reality's not holding up so well. Cause and effect are coming apart. Time's Worm has a bad case of being hypnotized, like the chicken, by the long white stripe in the middle of the road.

THOSE WHO CAN, DO

Brighde Mullins

Ann Marie, an idealistic poet, is driven out of teaching after being stalked by a student and harassed by a Dean. This speech takes place on the deck of the Staten Island Ferry, after Ann Marie has resigned her tenure track position and plans to return to her lucrative but soulless career in Advertising.

ANN MARIE. Yes, I fled. Yes. It was all a learning experience. One thing that I learned is that there is some validity in the well-worn phrase, the saying handed down. The phrase that cropped up for me, even as I was flailing was "no one is my enemy, no one is my friend, everyone is my teacher." It's a nice thought, anyway. Neutralizes the paranoia. Maybe that's what my shrink meant when she said that Celia freaked me out because of… *(Pause.)* I don't know. I am all right with Not Knowing. I don't need to know why she bothered me so much. Was she dangerous? Did I take her manias too personally? It's my life. I have to take it personally. *(Tiny beat.)* In Italy they call their teachers "maestro." In Ireland the teacher is the town hero. In Jewish culture the teacher is heaped with praise. In America you're the Village Idiot, the "One Who Can't," overworked, invisible until targeted, surrounded by the inept and saddled with the Walking Wounded, the casualties of an un-civilized civilization. I still take the Ferry some nights, just to feel the proximity of the moon, hear the screams of gulls, see the silhouette of the skyline. My idealism ended in a court-case, my career change ended in stretch marks, no matter! I learned some things. *(Little pause.)* I sit on the top deck of the Ferry. When it nudges into port in Staten Island, I don't get off. I wait. I simply wait. It will reverse direction. After ten minutes the heft of the ferry will churn back to Manhattan, where I still feel safe just walking around.

THREE SECONDS IN THE KEY

Deb Margolin

A Mother, suffering from Hodgkin's disease, recalls attempting to smoke medicinal pot.

MOTHER. You know, I can't smoke pot, I really can't. So many of my friends and colleagues have long enjoyed the benefits, the temporal and spiritual beauties of pot, the way it just extracts the diseased parts out of a moment and replaces them with silence or laughter, but I can't smoke it. It unzips me; some little silk pillow that holds all my hells and hierarchies rips open, and my mind pours out like mercury in little drops and just bounces. I can't smoke pot, I just can't get it done.

I temporarily forgot this aspect of my identity when they told me I had Hodgkin's disease. Two haughty and symmetrical glands swelled on either side of my neck; one went down, the other didn't. It's often like that in relationships! I was told to take this foolproof chemotherapy and get my life back. The doctor said it was a sword of Damocles, this Hodgkin's, which I could just move out of my way with some simple chemo, which was "very well tolerated" and "sure to work," and that's how this sacred mistake got made, with the pot.

The first time I smoked it was a sunny, radiant day in Autumn. With nausea running like a set of empty train tracks under every second of my experience, I felt like I had nothing to lose. A friend had brought me a joint up from Virginia, and I, the mortal little alchemist, just marched right into the bathroom and toked up. And here I am, just some weirdo who likes words! I came out of the bathroom and, although the air suddenly seemed to have holes in it like big pores in an old man's skin, and the furniture seemed warped and somehow on the verge of song, everything felt basically solid, and I went to the supermarket.

The supermarket! You have to be out of your mind! The supermarket! You must be crazy! Everything squeaked in the supermarket, and it was freezing cold and voguing as normal when in fact it was surfeited with useless objects and mumbling strangers and seemed like a rundown Greyhound bus terminal for inanimate objects or the criminally insane, and there was this demented music playing. But I carried on! I wanted to buy some fruit, so I wheeled my cart, which felt like an army jeep, into the produce area. The holes in the air got bigger, but I continued! I put my purse down next to a bunch of cantaloupes and honeydew melons to bend and pick up some onions or something and then, turning back to the melons, saw my purse among them, and was just blown away by the sight of it, lying just as valid as you please among melons, recontextualized in this surreal way, my purse just lying there among a bunch of melons, and I LOST IT! I started laughing and couldn't stop; tears came into my eyes and I tried to wipe them away but my glasses fell off, and I was groping to find them the way my Aunt Dodo used to grope for her false teeth when they fell out of her mouth during the Passover Seder, and this fit had me in its full grasp when a concerned shopper, seeing what must have looked like an epileptic seizure, came over to ask if I was all right, and just being seen by this woman in these circumstances set me off again, and I slid to the floor in a complete hysteria.

Actor's Choice: Monologues for Women

THREE SECONDS IN THE KEY

Deb Margolin

A Mother, suffering from Hodgkin's disease, analyzes each moment in terms of how much time they cost. She loves things that are dependent on time, like theater and basketball.

MOTHER. I'm just not sure about the time, that's all. I'm just not sure if I have any time. So I've become a time-shopper, a comparison-pricer, I browse the price of my ambitions in terms of how much time they cost. The phone rings: 9 minutes. Shower: 11 minutes. Crossword puzzle: 19 minutes. Supermarket for milk and eggs: 28 minutes. Making love: well…45 minutes. Rocking back and forth in anguishes of love for my children, in sorrow for the mountain of their future loss, in sudden, stabbing, quick flashes of contemplation of the parts of their lives which I may never see: weeks and weeks, days and days, hours and hours. I think that's why I'm most in love with art forms that are time dependent. I like music, which begins and ends in time. I like theater: when the last line is over, the light falls away from the bodies of the actors and the rain begins. I love the sound time makes, the huskiness or soprano of its passing.

Because for a while this is how we lived, my son and I, this is how we lived, out of time, we drank time out of a cup more than we lived in it, my staunch and pretty little boy and I, that is how we lived, and that cup was the television, a cup of time we sipped from as we lived outside it. Many things passed us by, but always without moving. Nothing moved for half a year. Some strange light stayed on us, in *Pieta,* my son and me, his head in my lap, the New York Knicks in a full season of struggle against themselves, for us and us alone; that is how we lived.

I love the Pieta. The dimension of time is exchanged for the dimension of suffering. It's hard to locate the suffering precisely, just like it's hard to notice the passage of time while it's happening. The body of the dead son is supposedly beyond suffering, but it twitches with its own resurrection; the body of the Mother, who has to be suffering terribly, is somehow peaceful beyond life, peaceful the way we say the dead are *at peace*.

THE TROPHY ROOM

Hilly Hicks, Jr.

Lisette was abandoned by her boyfriend Lewis when he got her pregnant. Lewis has died in the first Iraq war. She confronts Lewis's family.

LISETTE. I loved Lewis! I trusted him. *(Beat.)* I loved him so much, when I found out I was gon' be a mother, I wasn't even scared. I was happy. I was smiling and singing to myself. I wasn't worried at all. I went in my bedroom and locked the door. And I sat up in front of the mirror and took off my blouse. Took off my skirt. And I stared at myself, looking for the spot where I was gonna get big. I rubbed my hand over it. And over it. And over it. 'Til I thought I could feel my little baby in there… *(Beat.)* I wasn't gon' tell my mama about it. I was just gonna leave and not get her mad. But I wanted Lewis to come with me. I thought we were in love enough to be a family, so I asked him to come with me. *(A pause.)* But he didn't want the baby. He wanted me to give it up. "I wanna live a little more life, Lisette." I told him how happy the baby made me, but he didn't want anything to do with it. 'Cause he wanted to "live a little more life." So I told my mama. I told her I was in trouble… And she told me to leave…

TUMOR

Sheila Callaghan

Newly-pregnant Sarah is overwhelmed by a swarm of children when shopping for clothes to fit her former self.

SARAH. Walking around the women's department in Macy's. There are children everywhere, crawling like arachnids, they have more legs than I thought children were supposed to have but I guess you start to notice these things when you've been hijacked. Looking over their sweaty heads for something simple and angora I recall when angora was simple, when the angora gaze was not flecked with knots of unfiltered mess who run for no reason and stick to everything and wail like original sin multiplied by twelve.

I keep my eyes a safe distance above the swarming ick and spot a garment worthy of my once-upon self. I move towards it as smooth as a rollerball pen. Soon I am close enough to attract its static cling. My hand, electric, rises to the rising sweater arm, also electric, and in our dual reaching pose we are an Italian Renaissance masterpiece. But as my fingers splay for the grasp I feel an icy sludge make its way down my left leg.

I hear this: "It's not my fault, the bottom fell out!" And then a small person is galloping away from me towards a larger person. I look. My entire calf from knee to ankle is covered in a seeping red liquid. Pooling into the side of my sneaker is roughly eight ounces of bright red smashed ice. And lying next to my foot is a Slurpie cup with its bottom in shreds.

That night I dream of buckets and buckets of blood gushing from between my legs.

TUMOR

Sheila Callaghan

Gloria, in an attempt to soothe her pregnant patient, describes the procedure of having an abortion.

GLORIA. Welcome, Sarah. Are you here alone? That's fine. Don't be frightened. This is a common and relatively painless procedure. I'll describe it in detail. First, we give you a small amount of grain alcohol to loosen you up and get to know you a little better. Then we place a car jack beneath your bottom and hoist you right up. You'll most likely experience a slight bumping sensation. To gauge the size of your cavity we do something called the echo test, where we spread your legs and yell "hello" and count how many times our voice reverberates. Then we slick you up with raspberry jam and slide a tiny little Hoover vacuum into you, and after it a tiny little cleaning lady to operate the vacuum. She will run the vacuum in a spiral pattern around your womb until the floor is entirely clean. You may feel a little tickle here and there from the suction. Then we yank her out and wipe you down with some cotton balls, smack you on your ass and send you home. Nothing to it. Now, hold my hand, stop crying, and take a deep breath.

THE TYPOGRAPHER'S DREAM

Adam Bock

Margaret, a typographer, contemplates the effect typography has on the way we look at the world and how those who choose the types are capable of manipulating these interpretations.

MARGARET. Because if you look really closely at type, if you really look, if you really look closely at, you see that caps and small letters and numbers and punctuation, while they are the primary they're joined by secondary characteristics, small caps, accent marks, foreign punctuation marks like umlauts and ring accents and cedilla, and special signs like dollar signs and copyright marks and brackets, and suddenly as you keep looking, a whole landscape reveals itself. A landscape of voices and demands and sounds and Italics send the reader tilting into a dream world. A word in bold typeface shouts. It's it's And then you realize that this typeface is different from that one, it's more lyrical, it's rougher, it's more frank or the letters are spaced too far apart or the letters are too close together and and and And then you realize that there are all different kinds of typefaces and there are so many different ways they can all be used, and there must be so many different choices being made everywhere and all the time everywhere, and Someone has chosen this type over that one. Someone. Has chosen this one. It didn't just happen. And that's when people realize that how the text is shown is a choice, that someone has decided that this story should be told this way, should be shown to the world this way, not that. That this story would be better served by being told in a quiet tone of voice, or no rather instead it should be told loudly dramatically emphatically. And then, if they continue to wander along this thought path, people realize that one: all stories are told and two: how they are told is on purpose for a reason and three: that the truth is colored by the way it is told and four: that someone, someone hidden, has made a choice to color the truth this way and therefore it is no longer the truth and it's now just an opinion. Pretending to be the truth. If the typographer has done her job, this opinion will look like the truth.

(Pause.)

An unethical typographer can make lies look like the truth.

WHAT CORBIN KNEW

Jeffrey Hatcher

A cynical, sharp tongued woman regales two men with the tale of a book club meeting gone horribly awry.

THADA. Well, first I had to go to the post office and mail that story—I'm writing short stories again—and I was standing in line to get to this surly postal clerk who, when he sees me, says, "O.k., you're next," which is not what you want to hear from a postal worker. So, anyway, I mail the story, and I run to the bus so I can cover this book club lunch in Crescent Heights. It's the new trend. Guilt-ridden, middle class women, they read one book a week, then get together to discuss it. This week's book is Henry James' "Portrait of a Lady." Well, I like Henry James as much as the next person, who doesn't enjoy a sentence without a verb. So I get there, and the house is perfect, the hostess is gorgeous, her daughters all have these British names like Prunella and Cressida and Crudite. And then we meet the other "gals," these beautrons with bone structure. You could open beer bottles with their cheekbones. They've had so much plastic surgery their mouths meet at the backs of their necks. And one of them, Dorothy, is obviously so hung over, she's wearing sunglasses *in*side. Anyway, we sit down for lunch, which is low-fat cottage cheese and iced tea laced with, like, acid and PCPs, and then we go into the library, which my hostess points out has been organized by subject; I sense there's something fishy when I see they've got DEATH OF A SALES-MAN in with the murder mysteries. Then we sit in a circle and our hostess starts to give us background on Henry James, how he was from an important literary family, how he was an expatriate, how he was a "confirmed bachelor." Then we start in on the book, and I'm taking notes when about ten minutes into the discussion, the hostess comes out with the following. "I just didn't think Osmond was handsome." And they all nod, and she says, "Yes, Isabel's obsession is understandable in its *context*, but if you'd seen him in that movie where he kept trying to kill Clint Eastwood and the president you just knew he was trouble from the get-go." And I realize…they're talking about John Malkovich. And I know I should keep my mouth shut, but frankly I've had a few Thunderbird Ice Teas myself, and I blurt out: *"You didn't read the book! You're talking about the movie!"* And they stare at me like I've gutted a deer on the rug. And one of them, the one in the sunglasses, Dorothy, raises her hand and says, "I didn't see the movie, but I must say I liked the first side much better than the second." SHE HAD LISTENED TO THE AUDIO BOOK VERSION. I say: "You can't talk about novels you saw at the movies or heard in the car! Besides which, Henry James was not a 'Confirmed Bachelor,' he was a closet queen who had his first sexual encounter with the future Chief Justice of the United States Supreme Court Oliver Wendall Holmes who set him on the homosexual path for life. Why do you think they called him The Magnificent Yankee? And another thing, *Dorothy*, just because you listened to the audio tape, don't think you're better than the rest of them! A book is meant to be READ! You have to look at it. You have to absorb the type face. A work of literature is meant for the eyes!" And the hostess says: "Dorothy is blind." *(Beat.)* After that the discussion kind of petered out. Next week they're doing "Remembrance of Things Past." Audio Books has a tape that erases itself as you listen to it.

How was your day?

WHAT CORBIN KNEW

Jeffrey Hatcher

An angry wife rants about her professor husband's pseudo-professional relationships with his young, attractive female students and his obliviousness to her own wants and desires.

MARGO. Most women, if they thought for fifteen years that their husband was faithful, that he loved them, that he respected them, and then started to teach some phoney-baloney writing class and started molding the work of all these talented writers with all their original voices and their novel narrative devices and had to have coffee with them after class, maybe a drink, a walk,—and, oh yes, none of these talented voices are men, no *low, gruff* talented voices, just *high, chirpy* ones—and none of them are old or even middle aged or fat or homely, all these original, vivid, talented, novel voices happen to be *really hot looking*. And then if most women had to listen to him one night while he explained that he was in love with one of his students, some scrawny, little exposed nerve from Sarah Lawrence who is "trying to make the move from journalism to fiction," like that's *hard*, like "Wo! She *was* a potato farmer, *now* she's trying to move into micro-surgery!" Come on! *(Pause.)* And then you start complaining why don't I talk about politics and books and art, and why aren't I ambitious, and why don't I work at some cool little alternative weekly where I can write pretentious, obscure can't-give-a-fucks and have lots of free time to be neurotic and complain about my writing and my dead above the neck husband who's too stupid to notice that his wife is in love with her extension course teacher!

WONDERLAND

Brooke Berman

Mia, a quirky performance artist, is onstage performing a monologue about the similarities she and Marilyn Monroe share. With so much in common, including similar family histories, body types, and aspirations, Mia ponders about whether or not Marilyn Monroe also shared her obsession with food.

MIA. Do you think Marilyn Monroe had issues with sugar? Cravings for brownies? Or mint ice cream? Or just the frosting off the tops of cinnamon rolls and cupcakes? I mean, we all know about the champagne and the sleeping pills, but do you think that with all that *lusciousness*, sugar was ever an issue? See, I identify with Marilyn Monroe. We have the same body type. And, we both got dumped by our fathers and raised by crazy mothers, you know a similar family history, and so I think, anyway, that Marilyn Monroe and I probably crave the same things. Like stardom, for one, and reinvention and belonging and sexual attention, all that stuff. And neither one of us knows quite what to do with promptness or underwear. So, wouldn't it stand to follow that we'd both crave sugar?

I think about things like this every Monday night in my acting class. I take this acting class, and anyway, we have a new woman in class, and she bakes every week. Which means that I come to class and eat every week. Which means that by about nine o'clock every week I hit this feverish peak which could be how much I love acting or else just a sugar high, and I'm eating my seventh or eighth blondie one night obsessed with whether Marilyn Monroe could relate. You know what I mean, don't you?

Early in her career, Marilyn Monroe gave this interview in which she said, "I just want to be wonderful." The interviewer asked her what she wanted and she said, *I just want to be wonderful.* Well, yeah.

Me too. I just want to be wonderful too. Don't we all just want to be wonderful?

WONDERLAND

Brooke Berman

Mia, a performance artist, has just had her image repackaged by network executives and a toned-down, clichéd version of her life has been turned into a half-hour television show. Searching for answers during her existential crisis, Mia turns to the only option she has left: God. Inexperienced with praying and not quite sure how to address God, her prayer becomes more of an audition than a sincere confession.

MIA. Dear God. I can't believe I'm doing this.

Dear God. Wait. Am I supposed to be kneeling?

Oh, God—I mean, Dear God.

Okay, well number one, I have a problem with the God word. It sounds too much like Santa Claus or Daddy. Would it be okay if I change the words? Is it allowed? I mean, I just feel like I'm asking to talk to the person in charge, and isn't GOD a deeper thing than that?

Okay, Mia, you're expecting an answer here. Just, you know, trust your instincts. Okay. So. So, what do I call You? May I call you Guidance? Or Goodness? Or Source? Do I pray to the Angelic Realm? To the Wonder Twin Powers? Or to "Twin Peaks?" I don't know who to pray to, but I want to learn.

I am full of life and conflicting desires, full of restless thought and overindulgent mental activity, and it all keeps me from being simple.

My dreams are coming true, only it's different than I thought it would be, and now I'm looking for something else entirely to satisfy this longing inside. And Michael thinks I need to talk to You, only I don't know who You are. At least I don't think I do. So, please, Help me to know You.

And, Dear Whomever:

I want to be a movie star—I know I shouldn't want that, but I want that. There it is. That's what I want.

Thank you. Bless Camden and Michael and Grace and XL and all the casting people, the people in pre-production, the people in wardrobe, the writers and the PA's. Bless everyone.

Love, Mia.

Was that okay?

ACTOR'S CHOICE

HEIGHTS
04/09